MENCIUS

Other translations by David Hinton

The Analects

Chuang Tzu: The Inner Chapters

The Late Poems of Meng Chiao

The Selected Poems of Li Po

Landscape Over Zero *(Poems by Bei Dao)*

Forms of Distance *(Poems by Bei Dao)*

The Selected Poems of T'ao Ch'ien

The Selected Poems of Tu Fu

MENCIUS

Translated by David Hinton

COUNTERPOINT WASHINGTON, D.C.

First paperback edition 1999

Library of Congress Cataloging-in-Publication Data
Mencius.
[Meng-tzu. English]
Mencius / translated by David Hinton.
p. cm.
Includes bibliographical references.
ISBN 1-887178-62-7 (hc) — ISBN 1-58243-020-9 (pbk)
I. Hinton, David, 1954– . II. Title.
PL2478.P5413 1998
181'.112—dc21 98-30083
CIP

Printed in the United States of America on acid-free paper that meets the American National Standards Institute Z39-48 Standard.

Illustration: *Auspicious Grain,* Anonymous, Yüan Dynasty. Courtesy of the National Palace Museum, Taipei, Taiwan, Republic of China

Design and electronic production by David Bullen

COUNTERPOINT
P.O. Box 65793
Washington, D.C. 20035-5793

Counterpoint is a member of the Perseus Books Group.

10 9 8 7 6 5 4 3 2

FIRST PRINTING

Contents

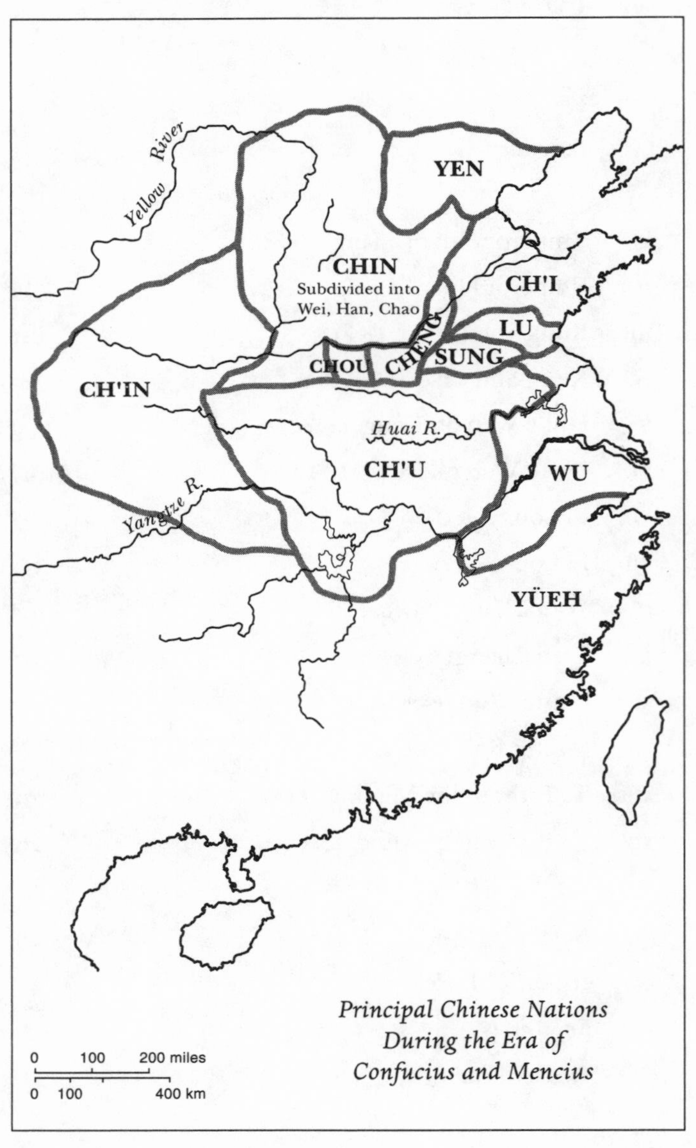

Principal Chinese Nations During the Era of Confucius and Mencius

Introduction

In a culture that makes no distinction between those realms we call the heart and the mind, Mencius was the great thinker of the heart. He was the second originary sage in the Confucian tradition, which has shaped Chinese culture for over two thousand years, and it was he who added the profound inner dimensions of human being to the Confucian vision.

In the ruins of a magisterial monotheism, a situation not entirely unlike our own, Confucius (551–479 B.C.E.) recognized society as a structure of human relationships, and spoke of those relationships as a system of "ritual" that people enact in their daily lives, thus infusing the secular with sacred dimensions. There is little sense of the inner self in Confucius' thought: identity is determined by a person's ritual roles in the social fabric, and this selflessness contributes deeply to the sense of human community as a sacred rite. The explicit realm of Confucius' teachings is occupied with the practical issues of how society works as a selfless weave of caring relationships; and in the implicit realm, that ritual weave is woven into the vast primal ecology of a self-generating and harmonious cosmos.

The Confucian social vision represents the end of a devastating, millennium-long transformation from a spiritualist to a humanist culture, and Mencius (4th c. B.C.E.) invested that humanist vision with its inner dimension by recognizing that the individual too is a part of the primal ecology. He saw all the spiritual depths of that cosmology inside us, and this led to a mystical faith in the inherent nobility of human beings. In his chaotic and war-ravaged times, he was therefore passionate in his defense of the people. Indeed, he advocated a virtual democracy in which a government's legitimacy depended upon the assent of the people. Such is the enduring magic of the Mencian heart – full of compassionate and practical concern for the human condition, and yet so empty that it contains the ten thousand transformations of the entire cosmos.

The tangible beginnings of Chinese civilization lie in the archaic Shang Dynasty (c. 1766–1040 B.C.E.), which bridged the transition from Neolithic to Bronze Age culture. (For an outline of the early dynasties and rulers that figure prominently in Mencius' writings, see Historical Table.) The Shang was preceded by the Neolithic Hsia Dynasty, about which very little is known. It appears that in the Paleolithic cultures that preceded the Hsia, nature deities were worshiped as tribal ancestors: hence a tribe may have traced its lineage back to an originary "High Ancestor River," for instance.

This practice apparently continued through the Hsia into the Shang, where evidence of it appears in oracle-bone inscriptions. Eventually, although these nature deities continued to be worshiped in their own right, religious life focused on the worship of human ancestors. By forging this religious system into a powerful form of theocratic government, the Shang was able to dominate China for no less than seven hundred years.

The Shang emperors ruled by virtue of their lineage, which was sanctified by Shang Ti ("Celestial Lord"), a supreme deity who functioned as the source of creation, order, ethics, etc. (*Shang* here represents two entirely different words in Chinese.) The Shang lineage may even have led to Shang Ti as its originary ancestor. In any case, Shang Ti provided the Shang rulers with a transcendental source of legitimacy and power: he protected and advanced their interests, and through their spirit-ancestors, they could decisively influence Shang Ti's shaping of events. All aspects of people's lives were thus controlled by the emperor: weather, harvest, politics, economics, religion, etc. Indeed, people didn't experience themselves as substantially different from spirits, for the human realm was simply an extension of the spirit realm.

Such was the imperial ideology, so convenient to the uses of power as it accorded little ethical value to the masses, who were not of select lineages. (Not surprisingly, the rise of Shang Ti seems to coincide with the rise of the Shang Dynasty, and later myth speaks of him as the creator of Shang civilization.) In the cruelest of ironies, it was overwhelming human suffering that brought the Chinese people into their earthly lives, beginning the transformation of this spiritualistic culture to a humanistic one. In the cultural legend, the early Shang rulers were paradigms of nobility and benevolence. But by the end of the Shang, the rulers had become cruel and tyrannical, and as there was no ethical system separate from the religious system, there was nothing to shield the people from their depredations. Meanwhile, a small nation was being pushed to the borders of the Shang realm by western tribes. This state of semi-barbarian people known as the Chou gradually adopted the cultural traits of the Shang. Eventually, under the leadership of the legendary sage-emperors Wen ("cultured") and Wu ("martial"), the Chou overthrew the tyrannical Shang ruler, thus founding the Chou Dynasty (1040–223 B.C.E.), which was welcomed wholeheartedly by the Shang people.

The Chou conquerors were faced with an obvious problem: if the Shang lineage had an absolute claim to rule the world, how could the Chou justify replacing it with their own, and how could they legitimize their rule in the eyes of the Shang people? Their solution was to redefine Shang Ti as *Heaven*, thus ending the Shang's claim to legitimacy by lineage, and then proclaim that the right to rule depended upon the Mandate of Heaven: once a ruler becomes unworthy, Heaven withdraws its mandate and bestows it on another. This was a major event in Chinese philosophy: the first investment of power with an ethical imperative. And happily, the early centuries of the Chou appear to have fulfilled that imperative admirably.

But eventually the Chou foundered because of its increasing inhumanity and its lack of the Shang's transcendent source of legitimacy: if the Mandate could be transferred to the Chou, it could obviously be transferred again. The rulers of the empire's component states (*chu hou:* "august lords") grew increasingly powerful, claiming more and more sovereignty over their lands, until finally they had established virtually independent nations. Eventually these rulers (properly called "dukes") even began assuming the title of emperor, thus equating themselves with the Chou emperor, who was by now a mere figurehead. The rulers of these autonomous states could at least claim descent from those who were first given the territories by the early Chou rulers. But this last semblance of legitimacy was also crumbling because these rulers were frequently at war with one another, which hardly inspired confidence in the claim that they were familial members of the ruling kinship hierarchy that was sanctioned by Heaven. More importantly, power was being usurped by a second tier of "august lords" whenever they had the strength to take it, and even by a third tier of high government officials. This history, beginning with the Chou's overthrow of the Shang, represents a geologic split in China's social structure: political power was breaking free of its family / religious context and becoming a separate entity.

The final result of the Chou's "metaphysical" breakdown was, not surprisingly, all too physical: war. In addition to constant pressure from barbarians in the north (the first devastating blow to Chou power was a barbarian invasion in 770 B.C.E.) and the Ch'u realm that dominated south China, there was relentless fighting between the empire's component states and frequent rebellion within them. This internal situation, so devastating to the people, continued to deteriorate after Confucius' time, until it finally gave an entire age its name: the Warring States Period (403–221 B.C.E.). Meanwhile, rulers caught up in this ruthless competition began looking for the most able men to help them rule their states, and this precipitated the rise of an independent intellectual class – a monumental event, for this class constituted the first open space in the cultural framework from which the imperial ideology could be challenged.

The old social order had now collapsed entirely, and

these intellectuals began struggling to create a new one. Although this was one of the most virulent and chaotic periods in Chinese history, it was the golden age of Chinese philosophy, for there were a "Hundred Schools of Thought" trying to envision what this new social order should be like. These schools were founded by thinkers who wandered the country with their disciples, teaching and trying to convince the various rulers to put their ideas into practice, for the desperate times had given them an urgent sense of political mission.

The first great figure of this intellectual class was Confucius, whose thought survives in a collection of aphoristic sayings entitled *The Analects*. Confucius' social philosophy derives from a rational empiricism, a methodology which Mencius shared and which represents a total break with Shang spiritualism. Blatant power-politics had made it impossible to believe in Heaven (let alone Shang Ti) as a transcendental source of order and legitimacy, so Confucius tried to rescue the fragmented Chou culture by putting it on a more viable rational and secular basis. He began from the empirical observation that human society is a structure, a weave of relationships between individuals who each occupy a certain locus in that structure: parent and child, ruler and subject, friend and friend, merchant and customer, and so forth. Confucius invested this anthropological observation with a philosophical dimension by recognizing that a vital community depends upon its members' fulfilling their communal responsibilities with an attitude of human caring. Always looking to the past as his source of wisdom, Confucius saw that societies flourished when their citizens (most especially their rulers) honored this moral principle, and inevitably crumbled when they ignored it: even the powerful transcendental glue of the Shang theocracy couldn't withstand the corrosive influence of the Shang emperors' depredations.

But Confucius' social philosophy goes well beyond this moral dimension, for he described the web of social responsibilities as a system of "Ritual" (*li:* see Key Terms). *Ritual* had been a religious concept associated with the worship of spirits, but Confucius extended its use to include all the caring acts by which we fulfill our responsibilities to others in the community. Hence, the entire weave of everyday social life takes on the numinous aspect of the sacred. There is little sense of the inner self in *The Analects:* the Ritual social fabric is paramount, and individual identity is defined entirely in terms of a person's social roles. All of the Confucian moral virtues (see Key Terms) apply only in the social context: one cannot speak of a person being virtuous in isolation. And there is indeed a kind of spiritual clarity in the self-

lessness of this Ritual weave, a clari
ing aspect in the structure of Chi
consciousness throughout the ag

Confucius located his human
that the Taoists described eloq
referred to only through silence:

> *Adept Kung said: "When the Master talks about civility and cultivation, you can hear what he says. But when he talks about the nature of things and the Way of Heaven, you can't hear a word."* *(V.12)*

A major component in that cosmology is the evolving concept of "Heaven." The most primitive meaning of *Heaven (t'ien)* is "sky." By extension, it also comes to mean "transcendence," for our most primal sense of transcendence may be the simple act of looking up into the sky. So it's hardly surprising that when the Chou wanted to reinvent Shang Ti in a more impersonal form, they would choose Heaven. By association with the idea of transcendence and that which is beyond us, it is natural that *Heaven* also comes to mean "fate" or "destiny." And this is precisely what we find in Confucius, where "destiny" has evolved out of the early Chou sense of an impersonal deity. But rather than destiny in the sense of a transcendental force deciding human fate, this is destiny as the inevitable evolution of

rding to the principles inherent in them. Al- Confucius focuses on its manifestations in human ry, there is little real difference between this Confucian eaven and that of the Taoists, who identified it with natural process proceeding according to the principle of *tzu-jan*. *Tzu-jan*'s literal meaning is "self-so" or "the of-itself" or "being such of itself," hence "spontaneous" or "natural." But a more descriptive translation might be "occurrence appearing of itself," for it is meant to describe the ten thousand things unfolding spontaneously, each according to its own nature. The Taoist ideal is to dwell as an organic part of the *tzu-jan* process. For Confucius, the mechanism of Heaven's process would be *tzu-jan*'s Confucian counterpart: *li* (Ritual). The Ritual structure of society is part of a much larger weave, the Ritual structure of natural process, and the Confucian ideal is for human community to dwell as an organic part of the cosmological weave of *li*.

The Confucian and Taoist Ways are traditionally described as the two poles of Chinese thought, but their shared cosmology affords them a fundamental unity, and that unity is no doubt why Chinese culture could eventually adopt both of these Ways simultaneously: the Confucian Way has defined the societal realm for Chinese intellectuals throughout the millennia, and the Way of philosophical Taoism has defined the private spiritual realm. The spiritual ecology of this shared cosmology might be seen as a return to the original spirituality of paleolithic China, for the sense of belonging to natural process is a secular version of the worship of nature deities as ancestral spirits. And it represents a complete secularization of the spiritualist regime that had dominated China since the rise of the Shang. Although ancestors continued to be attended assiduously, it was now a Confucian ritual of love and respect rather than an appeal to otherworldly powers. And although Confucius and Mencius recognized sacrifices to gods and spirits, they didn't necessarily believe any of the religious claims associated with such worship. For them, the value of such practices lay in the function they served in the Ritual structure of society. Mencius goes so far as to say that if gods and spirits don't fulfill human needs, they should be replaced (XIV.14). At the more fundamental level of the shared cosmology itself, it would appear to represent the resurgence of an ancient cosmology, a return to the culture's most primal roots – the Paleolithic and beyond. "Heaven" had become the current way of referring to its physical processes, and it was by recognizing the vast reach of Heaven within us that Mencius endowed the human with profound inner dimensions:

> *The ten thousand things are all there in me. And there's no joy greater than looking within and finding myself faithful to them.* (XIII.4)

This inner dimension also takes on ethical and political dimensions in Mencius' thought. Rather than privileged kinship relations as a basis of ethical value, Mencius proposes human belonging to the primal cosmology. Hence, citizens are all of equal value in and of themselves simply because they are all endowed with that vast reach of Heaven.

As with most intellectual figures in ancient China, very little is known of Mencius' life. He was born in Tsou, which was a dependency of Lu, the homeland of Confucius where the Chou cultural tradition was especially strong. His Chinese name was Meng K'o, and he is known as Meng Tzu, meaning "Master Meng," from which the latinized *Mencius* derives. According to tradition, he received his education first under the tutelage of a sagely mother and then under a disciple of Master Szu, who was Confucius' grandson and the reputed author of *The Doctrine of the Mean (Chung Yung)*, a book which came to be associated with the book of Mencius' writings, the *Mencius.* Sharing with most other philosophers of the time a faith in the political mission of the intellectual, he traveled with his disciples to the various states advising their rulers, hoping his ideas would be adopted and so lead to a more humane society. A number of rulers welcomed him, some even becoming benefactors, but his ideas were too radical and threatening. Few, if any, showed much inclination to put them into practice.

The book which bears Mencius' name probably represents the teachings of his mature thought. Unlike *The Analects,* which is largely made up of short aphoristic fragments without any supporting context, the *Mencius* is composed of longer and more developed passages, which makes it a fuller exposition of Confucian thought. It is entirely possible that Mencius wrote part or all of the book himself, though it is perhaps more likely that it was composed by his disciples. But if this is the case, it appears to be a compilation of carefully taken notes that represent pretty exactly the master's actual words. So, unlike *The Analects,* much of which is clearly not written by the historical Confucius, the *Mencius* seems almost entirely authentic. Indeed, it is considered a paragon of literary eloquence and style. The book contains fourteen chapters, arranged in seven pairs. Each pair shares the same title, which is taken from whatever personage happens to appear in the first sentence, a seemingly arbitrary method devised by a later editor. The only exception to this is the final pair: "To Fathom the Mind." This title, also drawn from the first sentence, is expressive of the unique character of these final chapters, for they seem to be an especially late and eloquent distillation of Mencius' ideas, containing many of his most striking and radical statements. An uncanny fact about Mencius is that his most distinctive and fundamental departures are found in only a handful of statements, which suggests that Mencius would appear an even more radical thinker if only more of his teachings had survived.

The inner dimension of human being was a central topic for the early Taoist masters, and they shared Mencius' cosmological view of the inner self; but for Mencius this was part of a political vision, and that is what makes him so important. As the human heart-mind is part of the fabric of Heaven, it is therefore inherently good and moral. Given this central belief in the inherent goodness of human nature, Mencius found the key to a flourishing society in a government that allows our inborn nobility to flourish of itself (here the similarity to Taoist thought is again unmistakable). And spiritual self-cultivation is the key both to that inner flourishing and to a benevolent government. The importance of self-cultivation among intellectuals was paramount in Confucius, who advocated government by a class of highly educated professionals. But in Mencius' cosmological context it takes on a decidedly spiritual dimension, reflecting the unity of self and cosmos:

> *To fathom the mind is to understand your nature. And when you understand your nature, you understand Heaven.* (XIV.1)

This idea of spiritual self-cultivation as a political act proved very appealing to the Neo-Confucianists of the Sung Dynasty. Although he was certainly influential, Mencius was not considered a preeminent figure until the rise of Neo-Confucianism, about 1,500 years after his death. Hoping to inspire people in the reconstruction of a beleaguered society, the Neo-Confucianists felt a need to give Confucian philosophy something of the spiritual depth that had made Buddhism (especially Ch'an or Zen Buddhism) so compelling in their culture. To do this they redefined the Confucian tradition by supplementing *The Analects* with three lesser-known texts which added a spiritual depth to Confucius' teachings, thus forming the canonical "Four Books": *The Analects, Mencius, The Great Learning,* and *The Doctrine of the Mean.* The Neo-Confucianists expanded Confucian self-cultivation to emphasize Ch'an meditation and the practice of the arts. Indeed, the monumental landscape painting that arose during the Sung was conceived in these Neo-Confucian terms: to look deeply into the ten thousand things is to look deeply into oneself. And, following Mencius, to look deeply into oneself is to look deeply into Heaven.

Given Mencius' faith in the inherent nobility of human beings, it is no surprise that he focuses so resolutely on the responsibility of rulers and intellectuals to create a society in which that nobility can flourish. For Mencius, the Mandate of Heaven is revealed through the will of the people:

> *Heaven sees through the eyes of the people. Heaven hears through the ears of the people.* (IX.5)

Indeed, the Mencian polity is a virtual democracy, for the emperor only has authority to rule so long as he has the people's approval. Once he loses their approval, he loses the Mandate of Heaven. Then, if they must, the people have every right to overthrow him.

The Mandate of Heaven remained the standard against which rulers were measured throughout the ages, though it was of course a standard they rarely met. Two millennia after Mencius, rulers of dubious repute felt compelled to commission paintings like *Auspicious Grain* (see jacket illustration), as if they could mask reality by associating themselves with a monumental totemic image representing the people's prosperity under a ruler who is fulfilling the Mandate of Heaven. However rare the society it depicts may be, it is indeed a beautiful image: a sacred human community flourishing in the shimmering weave of Heaven's natural process.

1

EMPEROR HUI OF LIANG *Book One*

1 Mencius went to see Emperor Hui of Liang, and the emperor said: "Even a thousand miles[1] wasn't too great a journey for you. You must come bringing something of great profit to my nation."

"Don't talk about profit," said Mencius. "It's Humanity[2] and Duty[3] that matter. Emperors say *How can I profit my nation?* Lords say *How can I profit my house?* And everyone else says *How can I profit myself?* Then everyone high and low is scrambling for profit, pitching the nation into grave danger.

"If the ruler in a nation of ten thousand war-chariots is killed, the assassin is no doubt lord to a house of a thousand war-chariots. And if the ruler in a nation of a thousand war-chariots is killed, the assassin is no doubt lord to a house of a hundred war-chariots. A thousand in ten thousand or a hundred in a thousand – this is no small amount. But when people betray Duty and crave profit, they aren't content until they've got it all. If they aren't Humane, they'll abandon their kindred, and if they aren't Dutiful, they'll betray their ruler.

"Just talk about Humanity and Duty, and leave it at that. Don't talk about profit."

2 Mencius went to see Emperor Hui of Liang and found him standing beside a pool. Gazing at the deer and wild geese, the emperor said: "And do the wise also enjoy such things?"

"Only the wise can enjoy them," replied Mencius. "If they aren't wise, even people who have such things can't enjoy them. *The Book of Songs* says:

> *He planned the sacred tower and began.*
> *He planned it well and managed it well,*
> *and the people worked with devotion,*
> *so it was finished in less than a day.*
> *He planned and began without haste,*
> *and the people were children coming.*
> *With the emperor in the sacred gardens*
> *there, the deer lay in pairs at ease,*
> *paired deer all sleek and glistening,*
> *white birds all bright and shimmering,*
> *and with the emperor at the sacred pool*
> *there, the fish leapt so strong and sure.*

Emperor Wen[4] used the people's labor to build his tower and his pool, and yet the people delighted in them. They called the tower *Sacred Tower* and the pool *Sacred Pool,* and they were delighted that he had deer and fish and turtles. The ancients knew joy because they shared their joy with the people.

"In *The Declaration of T'ang,* the tyrant Chieh's people say: *When will you founder, o sun? We'll die with you gladly.* The people so hated him that they thought dying with him was better than living with him. He had towers and ponds, birds and animals – but how could he enjoy them alone?"

3 Emperor Hui of Liang said: "I've devoted myself entirely to the care of my nation. If there's famine north of the river, I move people east of the river and grain north of the river. And if there's famine east of the river, I do the opposite. I've never seen such devotion in the governments of neighboring countries, but their populations are growing by leaps and bounds while mine hardly grows at all. How can this be?"

"You're fond of war," began Mencius, "so perhaps I could borrow an analogy from war. War drums rumble, armies meet, and just as swords clash, soldiers throw down their armor and flee, dragging their weapons behind them. Some run a hundred feet and stop. Some run fifty feet and stop. Are those who run fifty feet justified in laughing at those who run a hundred feet?"

"No, of course not," replied the emperor. "It's true they didn't run the full hundred feet, but they still ran."

"If you understood this, you wouldn't long to have more

people than neighboring countries. Look – when growing seasons aren't ignored, people have more grain than they can eat. When ponds aren't plundered with fine-weave nets, people have more fish and turtles than they can eat. When mountain forests are cut according to their seasons, people have more timber than they can use. When there's more grain and fish than they can eat, and more timber than they can use, people nurture life and mourn death in contentment. People nurturing life and mourning death in contentment – that's where the Way of emperors begins.

"When every five-acre[5] farm has mulberry trees around the farmhouse, people wear silk at fifty. And when the proper seasons of chickens and pigs and dogs are not neglected, people eat meat at seventy. When hundred-acre farms never violate their proper seasons, even large families don't go hungry. Pay close attention to the teaching in village schools, and extend it to the child's family responsibilities – then, when their silver hair glistens, people won't be out on roads and paths hauling heavy loads. Our black-haired people free of hunger and cold, wearing silk and eating meat at seventy – there have never been such times without a true emperor.

"But you don't think about tomorrow when people are feeding surplus grain to pigs and dogs. So when people are starving to death in the streets, you don't think about emptying storehouses to feed them. People die, and you say *It's not my fault, it's the harvest*. How is this any different from stabbing someone to death and saying *It's not me, it's the sword*? Stop blaming harvests, and people everywhere under Heaven will come flocking to you."

4 Emperor Hui of Liang said: "I'm ready to be taught without resenting it."

"Is there any difference between killing someone with a stick or killing them with a sword?" began Mencius.

"No, there's no difference."

"And killing with a sword or a government – any difference?"

"No difference."

"There's plenty of juicy meat in your kitchen and plenty of well-fed horses in your stable," continued Mencius, "but the people here look hungry, and in the countryside they're starving to death. You're feeding humans to animals. Everyone hates to see animals eat each other, and an emperor is the people's father and mother – but if his government feeds humans to animals, how can he claim to be the people's father and mother?

"When Confucius said *Whoever invented burial figures deserved no descendants,* he was condemning the way people make human figures only to bury them with the dead. But that's nothing compared to the way you're pitching your people into starvation."

5 Emperor Hui of Liang said: "As you know, this country was once the strongest anywhere under Heaven. But here I am: defeated by Ch'i in the east, my eldest son dead in the battle; seven hundred square miles[6] lost to Ch'in in the west; and humiliated by Ch'u in the south. Now, out of respect for the dead, I long to wash all this shame away. How can I do that?"

"To be a true emperor, even a hundred square miles can be land enough," replied Mencius. "If an emperor's rule is Humane – punishment and taxation are light, people plow deep and hoe often, and strong men use their leisure time to cultivate themselves as sons and brothers, loyal subjects and trustworthy friends. They serve father and brother when home, and when away they serve elders and superiors. So even with nothing but sticks for weapons, they can overcome the fierce swords and armor of nations like Ch'in or Ch'u.

"In such countries, emperors violate the proper seasons of their people. They don't let them plow or weed or tend to their parents. Parents are cold and hungry, brothers and wives and children are scattered far apart. Those emperors are dragging their people down into ruin. So if a true emperor invaded their countries, who would oppose him? Therefore it is said: *No one can oppose the Humane.* If only you would believe this."

6 Mencius went to see Emperor Hsiang of Liang.[7] Talking with someone after he'd left, he said: "At first sight, he didn't seem like much of a sovereign, and after meeting him I saw nothing to command respect. But suddenly he began asking questions.

"*What could bring stability to all beneath Heaven?* he asked.

"*In unity is stability,* I replied.

"*Who can unify all beneath Heaven?*

"*One who has no lust for killing.*

"*But who would give it all to him?*

"*Is there anyone who wouldn't give it to him? Don't you know about rice shoots? If there's a drought in the sixth or seventh month, rice shoots wither. But if the Heavens then fill with clouds, and rain falls in sheets, the shoots burst into life again. When this happens, who can resist it? Today, all of the world's great shepherds share a lust for killing. If there were someone free of that lust, people everywhere under Heaven would crane their necks watching for him to come. And if such a man really appeared, the people going home to him would be like a flood of water pouring down. Who could resist it?"*

7 Emperor Hsüan of Ch'i said: "I'd like to hear about Duke Huan[8] of Ch'i and Duke Wen of Chin."

"The disciples of Confucius never spoke of Huan or Wen," replied Mencius, "so their histories weren't passed down through the generations, and I've heard nothing of them. You won't learn much about the true emperor from them."

"Tell me then – this Integrity[9] that makes a true emperor, what is it?" asked Emperor Hsüan.

"If you watch over the people, you're a true emperor and nothing can resist you."

"Can someone like me watch over the people?"

"Yes."

"How do you know this?"

"I heard a story about you from Hu He: *Sitting in the palace one day, the emperor saw some people leading an ox past outside.*

"'*Where's that ox being taken?*' he asked.

"'*We're going to consecrate the new bell with its blood.*'

"'Let it go. I can't bear to see it shivering with fear like an innocent person being hauled off to the executioner.'

"'Then shall we leave the bell unconsecrated?'

"'No, no – that would never do. Use a sheep instead.' Did that really happen?"

"Yes," replied the emperor.

"You have the heart of a true emperor. The people all thought you were being miserly. But I know you just couldn't bear the suffering."

"Are the people really like that? Ch'i may be a small country, but how could I begrudge a single ox? I just couldn't bear to see it shivering with fear like an innocent person being hauled off to the executioner. So I told them to use a sheep instead."

"It isn't so strange that the people thought you miserly," said Mencius. "You wanted to use a small animal instead of a large one, so how were they to know? If you were so grieved by something innocent going to the executioner, then what's the difference between an ox and a sheep?"

The emperor laughed and said: "What was going on in this heart of mine? I certainly didn't begrudge the expense of an ox, but I wanted to use a sheep instead. No wonder the people called me a miser."

"No harm done," said Mencius. "That's how Humanity works. You'd seen the ox, but not the sheep. And when noble-minded people see birds and animals alive, they can't bear to see them die. Hearing them cry out, they can't bear to eat their meat. That's why the noble-minded stay clear of their kitchens."

After a moment, the emperor spoke: "The *Songs* say

> *It's another person's heart,*
> *but mine has fathomed it.*

This describes you perfectly. It was I who did these things, but when I turned inward in search of motives, I couldn't fathom my own heart. It was you who explained it, and only then did I come to this realization. So how can this heart of mine be that of a true emperor?"

"What if someone said this to you: *I'm strong enough to lift a thousand pounds, but I can't lift a feather?* Or: *My sight's so good I can see the tip of an autumn hair, but I can't see a cartload of firewood?* Would you believe it?"

"No, of course not."

"You have compassion enough for birds and animals, but you do nothing for your people. And why is that? When feathers can't be lifted, someone isn't using their strength. When a cartload of firewood can't be seen, someone isn't using their sight. And when the people aren't watched over, someone isn't using their compassion. So if you aren't a true emperor, it's only because you're unwilling, not because you're incapable."

"The unwilling and the incapable – is there any difference in form?" asked the emperor.

"You can say that you're incapable of bounding over the North Sea with T'ai Mountain tucked under your arm, and in fact you are incapable. You can also say that you're incapable of breaking up a little kindling for an old woman, but in fact you're unwilling, not incapable. Your failure to be a true emperor isn't like failing to bound over the North Sea with T'ai Mountain tucked under your arm. It's like failing to break up a little kindling for an old woman.

"Honor your own elders as befits elders, and extend this honor to all elders. Honor your own children as befits children, and extend this honor to all children. Then you can turn all beneath Heaven in the palm of your hand.

"The *Songs* say:

Setting an example for his wife
and extending it to his brothers,
he ruled both home and country,

which describes how this heart here can be applied elsewhere. Just do that and your compassion will be expansive enough to watch over all within the four seas. If your compassion isn't expansive, you can't even watch over your own wife and child. This is precisely why the ancients so completely surpassed the rest of us: they made whatever they did expansive. That's all. You have compassion enough for birds and animals, but you do nothing for your people. And why is that?

"To know whether something is light or heavy, you must weigh it. To know whether something is long or short, you must measure it. It's like this for all things, and especially for the heart. If only you would measure yours.

"Or perhaps you want to keep sending out your armies with their armor and swords, endangering your subjects and stirring up hatred among the other rulers. Is that what fills your heart with delight?"

"No," replied the emperor. "How could I delight in that? I only do it for the sake of a great dream."

"And this great dream – may I hear what it is?"

The emperor just smiled and said nothing.

"Is your grand cuisine not enough for your tongue? Are your summer and winter robes not enough for your body? Perhaps all the beautiful sights here aren't enough for your eyes, and the beautiful music isn't enough for your ears? Or is it that your attendants aren't fine enough to serve you? But you have many assistants and advisors: whatever you find wanting, they can supply. So this can't be the kind of dream you harbor."

"No," replied the emperor, "it isn't."

"Then it isn't hard to guess what your great dream is. You dream of more land. You dream of Ch'in and Ch'u paying court to you, of ruling over the entire Middle Kingdom[10] and pacifying the barbarian nations on all four borders. Doing the kinds of things you do in search of such a dream – that's like climbing a tree in search of a fish."

"Is it really so bad?" asked the emperor.

"Yes, and it's much more dangerous," replied Mencius. "Climb a tree in search of a fish, and though you won't find a fish, you also won't find disaster. But do the kinds of things you do in search of your dream, and though you wear body and mind ragged, you'll find disaster for sure."

"Please – can you tell me more about this?"

"If Chou and Ch'u went to war, who do you think would win?"

"Ch'u would win."

"So the small is clearly no match for the large," continued Mencius, "the few is clearly no match for the many, and the weak is clearly no match for the strong. Here within the vast seas, there are nine regions, each spreading a thousand square miles, and your Ch'i is but one of them. To conquer eight with one, how is that any different from Chou declaring war on Ch'u?

"You must return to fundamentals. If you were renowned for Humane government, every scholar under Heaven would long to stand in your court, every farmer would long to plow in your countryside, every merchant would long to trade in your markets, every traveler would long to travel your roads, and everyone beneath Heaven who despised their rulers would long to rush here and confide in you. If you made this happen, who could resist it?"

"I'm not all that bright," said the emperor. "I still can't see my way through this. But I'm determined and want your help. If you'll explain clearly, perhaps I can learn, and even though I'm not terribly clever, I'll try to act on your counsel."

"To keep the mind constant without a constant livelihood – only the wisest among us can do that. Unless they have a constant livelihood, the common people will never have constant minds. And without constant minds, they'll wander loose and wild. They'll stop at nothing, and soon cross the law. Then, if you punish them accordingly, you've done nothing but snare the people in your own trap. And if they're Humane, how can those in high position snare their people in traps? Therefore, in securing the people's livelihood, an enlightened ruler ensures that they have enough to serve their parents and nurture their wives and children, that everyone has plenty to eat in good years and no one starves in bad years. If you do that, you'll be leading the people toward virtue and benevolence, so it will be easy for them to follow you.

"But now, with you securing their livelihood, the people never have enough to serve their parents or nurture their wives and children. In good years they live miserable lives, and in bad years they starve to death. All they can do is struggle to stay free of death and worry about failing. Where could they ever find the leisure for Ritual[11] and Duty?

"If you want to put my words into practice, why not return to fundamentals? When every five-acre farm has mulberry trees around the farmhouse, people wear silk at fifty. And when the proper seasons of chickens and pigs and dogs are not neglected, people eat meat at seventy. When hundred-acre farms never violate their proper seasons, even large families don't go hungry. Pay close attention to the teaching in village schools, and extend it to the child's family responsibilities – then, when their silver hair glistens, people won't be out on roads and paths hauling heavy loads. Our black-haired people free of hunger and cold, wearing silk and eating meat in old age – there have never been such times without a true emperor."

II

EMPEROR HUI OF LIANG *Book Two*

1 Chuang Pao went to see Mencius and said: "I went to see the emperor, and he told me that he loves music. I didn't know what to say. *Loving music* – what do you think of that?"

"If the emperor truly loves music," replied Mencius, "there may be hope for Ch'i."

Some days later, Mencius went to see the emperor and asked: "Is it true you told Chuang that you love music?"

The emperor blushed and said: "I cannot claim to love the music of ancient emperors, only our own trifling music."

"If you truly love music," said Mencius, "there may be hope for Ch'i. And it makes no difference if it's today's music or the music of ancient times."

"Please – can you tell me more about this?" asked the emperor.

"To enjoy music alone or to enjoy it with others," began Mencius, "which is the greater pleasure?"

"With others, of course," replied the emperor.

"And to enjoy music with a few or to enjoy it with many – which is the greater pleasure?"

"With many, of course."

"Can I tell you about enjoyment? Suppose there was a performance of beautiful music here. Suppose the people heard the sound of their emperor's bells and drums, pipes and flutes, and turning faces furrowed with worry toward each other, they said: *Why does our emperor let his love of music make our lives so desperate – father and son, brother and brother, mother and child all separated and scattered apart?* Suppose there was a hunt ranging through the fields here. Suppose the people heard the sound of your carriages and horses, saw the beauty of your banners and streamers, and turning faces furrowed with worry toward each other, they said: *Why does our emperor let his love of hunting make our lives so desperate – father and son, brother and brother, mother and child all separated and scattered apart?*

"There could be only one explanation for all this: never sharing pleasure with the people.

"But suppose there was a performance of beautiful music here. Suppose the people heard the sound of their emperor's bells and drums, pipes and flutes, and turning happy faces full of delight toward each other, they said: *Listen – they're making music, so our emperor must be feeling fine!* And suppose there was a hunt ranging through the fields here. Suppose the people heard the sound of your carriages and horses, saw the beauty of your banners and streamers, and turning happy faces full of delight toward each other, they said: *Look – they're out hunting, so our emperor must be feeling fine!*

"There could be only one explanation for all this: sharing pleasure with the people. Sharing pleasure with the people – that's what makes an emperor an emperor."

2 Emperor Hsüan of Ch'i asked: "Is it true that Emperor Wen's park covered seventy square miles?"

"The *Chronicles* say it did," replied Mencius.

"Was it really so vast?"

"To the people it seemed small."

"My park covers only forty square miles, and yet the people consider it huge," said the emperor. "How can this be?"

"Emperor Wen's park may have covered seventy square miles, but it was open to the people: they gathered dry grasses for their fires there, they hunted pheasants and rabbits there. He shared it with the people, so is it any wonder the people considered it small?

"When I first came to the borders of your nation, I asked about the great prohibitions of this land. Only then did I dare enter. I was told that there is a park covering forty square miles, and that anyone who kills a deer there is punished as if they'd killed a person. So this park is a forty-square-mile trap set in the middle of the country. Is it any wonder the people consider it huge?"

3 Emperor Hsüan of Ch'i asked: "Is there a Way[1] to foster good relations with neighboring countries?"

"There is," replied Mencius. "Only a person of great Humanity can use the large to serve the small. So it is that Emperor T'ang served Ko and Emperor Wen served the K'un tribes. Only a person of great wisdom can use the small to serve the large. So it is that Emperor T'ai[2] served the Hsün-yü tribes and Kou Chien served the nation of Wu.

"Whoever uses the large to serve the small delights in Heaven. Whoever uses the small to serve the large fears Heaven. If you delight in Heaven, you nurture all beneath Heaven. If you fear Heaven, you nurture your own nation. The *Songs* say:

> *Fearing august Heaven's majesty,*
> *we nurture our nation forever."*

"Your words are great indeed," said the emperor. "But I have a weakness: I love valor."

"Then let it not be small valor that you love. That is to

clutch your sword and glare angrily, shouting *How dare he oppose me?* It's such coarse valor – at best useful only against a lone opponent. Let it be great valor that you love.

"The *Songs* say:

> *Majestic in his fury and wrath,*
> *the emperor marshalled his forces.*
> *He met the invaders in Chü*
> *and secured Chou's prosperity,*
> *fulfilling all beneath Heaven.*

Such is the valor of Emperor Wen. In a single act of wrath, he brought peace to the people throughout all beneath Heaven.

"The *Book of History* says: *Heaven sent down people. It created a sovereign for them and made him their teacher, saying 'You must help the Celestial Lord*[3] *show his love for them. To every corner of the land, I will judge those who offend and those who do not. In all beneath Heaven, who will dare cast their ambition against my purpose?'*

"There was only one man causing trouble in all beneath Heaven, but Emperor Wu[4] took it as a personal disgrace. Such is the valor of Emperor Wu. In a single act of wrath, he too brought peace to the people throughout all beneath Heaven.

"Now if you too, in a single act of wrath, bring peace to the people throughout all beneath Heaven, the people's only fear will be that your love of valor may end."

4 Emperor Hsüan of Ch'i received Mencius in the Snow Palace and said: "Does the sage also enjoy such pleasures?"

"Yes," replied Mencius. "Denied such pleasures, there are those who would malign their sovereign. To malign a sovereign because you're denied such pleasures is wrong. But when a sovereign fails to share such pleasures with his people – that too is wrong. If you delight in the people's pleasure, the people will delight in your pleasure. If you worry over the people's troubles, the people will worry over your troubles. Make all beneath Heaven your delight and all beneath Heaven your worry – then how can you fail to be a true emperor?

"Long ago, Duke Ching of Ch'i asked his prime minister, Lord Yen: *I long to visit Chuan-fu Mountain and Ch'ao-wu Mountain, then travel along the coastline south to Lang-yeh Mountain. What can I do to make my travels rival those of the ancient emperors?*

"*What a fine question,* replied Lord Yen. *When the Son of Heaven visited the august lords, it was called an Inspection Tour because he was inspecting the territories under their care. And when the august lords went to the Son of Heaven's court, it was called a Duty Report because they reported on how they had carried out their duties. These things were not done without a purpose. In spring, it was to inspect the planting and provide whatever the farmers lacked. And in autumn, it was to inspect the harvest and help whoever didn't bring in enough. In the Hsia Dynasty there was a saying:*

> *If our emperor doesn't journey*
> *where will we find rest?*
> *If our emperor doesn't tour,*
> *where will we find help?*
> *Each journey, each tour,*
> *he's a model for august lords.*

"It's not like that anymore. Now

> *marching armies demand supplies,*
> *so there's no food for the hungry*
> *and no rest for the work-weary.*
> *Looking away, voices full of hate,*
> *the people turn to shadowy crime.*
> *Defying the mandate, rulers abuse us.*
> *They drift, awash in food and drink.*
> *Adrift, unbridled, wild, wanton:*
> *among lords this means trouble.*

To follow the drift downstream, all thought of return gone: that is called adrift. To follow the drift upstream, all thought of return gone: that is called unbridled. To follow animals, all moderation gone: that is called wild. To wallow in wine, all moderation gone: that is called wanton. The early emperors never indulged in pleasures adrift and unbridled, or actions wild and wanton.

"It is for you to choose your path.

"Duke Ching was overjoyed. He issued great proclamations throughout the land, then he went to live in a hut outside the city. He opened the granaries to those in need, and summoned his Grand Music-master, saying: *Compose for me the joyous harmony of sovereign and subject.* Hence the *Chih Shao* and *Chüeh Shao,* with lyrics saying: *How can guiding the sovereign be a crime?* To guide the sovereign is to love the sovereign."

5 Emperor Hsüan of Ch'i said: "Since I never use it, people all tell me I should tear down the Palace of Light. Should I tear it down or not?"

"It's the Palace of Light because it's the palace of an emperor," replied Mencius. "If you want to govern as a true emperor, don't tear it down."

"*To govern as a true emperor* – could you explain this for me?"

"In ancient times, when Emperor Wen ruled Ch'i[5] – farmers were taxed one part in nine, descendants of worthy officials were insured a livelihood, there were inspections at border crossings and markets but no taxes, fish traps were not regulated, criminals were punished but not their families.

"Old men without wives we call widowers. Old women without husbands we call widows. Old people without children we call loners. Children without fathers we call orphans. These four kinds of people – they are the forsaken ones of this world. They have no one to turn to. When Emperor Wen's rule spread Humanity throughout the land, he put these four kinds of people above all else. The *Songs* say:

> *While the rich manage in fine fashion,*
> *the forsaken nurture no hope, no hope.*

"Your words are fine indeed," said the emperor.

"You call them fine, but in practice you ignore them. Why is that?"

"I have a weakness," replied the emperor. "I love the bounty of wealth."

"In ancient times, Emperor Kung Liu[6] loved the bounty of wealth," said Mencius. "But the *Songs* say:

> *He filled granaries with stores,*
> *bundled supplies and provisions*

into sacks and well-stocked bags.
His splendor spreading repose,
he kept archers in plain sight,
flourished spear, shield, and ax.
Only then did his march begin.

Hence, those who stayed had granaries full of stores, and those who went had bags well stocked. Only then could he begin his march to settle a homeland. If you love the bounty of wealth, let it be the people's love too – then how will it keep you from being a true emperor?"

"I have another weakness," said the emperor. "I love beauty and passion."

"In ancient times," replied Mencius, "Emperor T'ai also loved beauty and passion. He adored the palace courtesans. But the *Songs* say:

Our true old father T'ai
came early on his horse,
skirting a western river
to reach Ch'i Mountain,
and with Lady Chiang
founded our homeland.

At that time, women never languished without husbands, nor men without wives. If you love beauty and passion – let it be the people's love too, then how will it keep you from being a true emperor?"

6 Mencius said to Emperor Hsüan of Ch'i: "Suppose one of your ministers entrusts his family to the care of a friend and then leaves on a journey to Ch'u. When he returns, he finds that the friend abandoned his family to hunger and cold. What should be done?"

"End the friendship," replied the emperor.

"And if a chief judge can't govern his court – what should be done?"

"Turn him out," pronounced the emperor.

"And if someone can't govern this land stretching out to the four borderlands – what then?"

The emperor suddenly turned to his attendants and spoke of other things.

7 Mencius went to see Emperor Hsüan of Ch'i and said: "If a nation is called ancient, it isn't because the trees there are tall. It's because the ministers there are descended from generations of high officials. But there's no sense of old family bonds between you and your ministers. Those you promote one day are gone the next, and you hardly notice."

"But how can I recognize mediocrity and avoid it?" asked the emperor.

"To advance only the wise," replied Mencius, "a sovereign often promotes the common above the august, the distant above the familial. In deciding who is worthy, always remain cautious. When your attendants all say someone is wise, that doesn't make him worthy. When your high ministers all say someone is wise, that doesn't make him worthy. When everyone in the country says someone is wise, investigate thoroughly. If you find that he is indeed wise and worthy, take him into your government.

"When your attendants all say someone is unworthy, don't listen. When your high ministers all say someone is unworthy, don't listen. When everyone in the country says someone is unworthy, investigate thoroughly. If you find that he is indeed unworthy, turn him out.

"When your attendants all say someone deserves death, don't listen. When your high ministers all say someone deserves death, don't listen. When everyone in the country says someone deserves death, investigate thoroughly. If you find that he does indeed deserve death, put him to death. Then it will be said *The entire country put him to death.*

"If it's like this in your country, you've truly become mother and father to the people."

8 Emperor Hsüan of Ch'i asked: "Is it true that Emperor T'ang banished the tyrant Chieh, and Emperor Wu overthrew the tyrant Chou?"[7]

"Yes, according to the histories," replied Mencius.

"So is the murder of a sovereign acceptable?"

"A thief of Humanity is called a thief," replied Mencius. "A thief of Duty is called a felon. Someone who's both a thief and a felon is called a commoner. I've heard of the commoner Chou's punishment, but I've never heard of a sovereign's murder."

9 Talking with Emperor Hsüan of Ch'i, Mencius said: "To build a grand home, you must send the master carpenter in search of huge trees. If he finds them, you'll be pleased and consider him truly capable. But if the workers then cut them into small pieces, you'll be angry and consider them truly inept.

"When grown, we're anxious to put our youthful learning to use. But what if an emperor says *Put aside what you've learned and obey me*? If you have a piece of jade, even if it's worth ten thousand *yi* in gold, you need to trust a jade-carver to cut and polish it for you. And in governing the nation – if you say *Put aside what you've learned and obey me,* how is that any different from trying to teach the jade-carver how to cut jade?"

10 After Ch'i invaded the nation of Yen and conquered it,[8] Emperor Hsüan said: "Some say I shouldn't annex Yen, and some say I should. For a nation of ten thousand war-chariots to conquer a nation of ten thousand war-chariots in only fifty days – human strength alone cannot perform such feats. If I don't annex Yen, Heaven will surely be offended and send down calamities. But if I do – what then?"

"If annexation will please the Yen people," replied Mencius, "then do it. There are examples of this among the ancients: Emperor Wu, for instance. And if annexation won't please the Yen people, then don't do it. There are also examples of this among the ancients: Emperor Wen, for instance.

"If a nation of ten thousand war-chariots invades another nation of ten thousand war-chariots, and the invader is welcomed with baskets of food and jars of wine, there can be only one reason: the people are fleeing fire and flood. But if the flood just gets deeper and the fire hotter, they'll no doubt turn again."

11 When Ch’i invaded Yen and annexed it, the other emperors began plotting Yen’s rescue.

Emperor Hsüan said: “The other emperors are planning to invade. What shall I do?”

“I’ve heard of having seventy square miles and ruling all beneath Heaven,” replied Mencius. “Emperor T’ang is an example. But I’ve never heard of ruling a thousand square miles and cowering in fear of others.

“The *Book of History* says: *Emperor T’ang’s expeditions began in Ko*. There he gained the trust of all beneath Heaven – so when he marched east, the western tribes complained. And when he marched south, the northern tribes complained: *Why does he leave us for last?* People watched for him the way they watched for rain in the midst of a great drought. When he came, they went to market unhindered again and tended their fields without interference. He punished the rulers and comforted the people, like rain falling in its season. And so, a great joy rose among the people. The *Book of History* also says: *We’re waiting for our lord: his coming will bring us back to life*.

“Now the Yen emperor tyrannized his people, so you attacked him. The people thought they were being rescued from fire and flood, so they welcomed you with baskets of food and jars of wine. How can you justify killing elders and taking the young captive, tearing down temples and stealing sacred vessels? The power of Ch'i was already feared throughout all beneath Heaven, and now you've doubled your territory without making your government Humane. No wonder all beneath Heaven is up in arms.

"Hurry! Send out orders to release old and young, to leave the sacred vessels where they are. Consult the people of Yen, appoint a new ruler, and then leave. There's still time to prevent this invasion."

12 There was a battle on the border between Chou and Lu.

"I lost thirty-three officials," complained Duke Mu of Chou, "but not one of my people died. There are too many to punish. But if I don't punish them, I'll be condoning what they did: watching their leaders die without lifting a finger to help. What can I do?"

"In years of calamity and failed harvests," replied Mencius, "how many thousands of your people suffered – young and old alike abandoned to gutters and ditches, the strong scattered to every corner of the land? Meanwhile, your granaries were full and your storehouses well stocked. Your officers kept all this from you, thus disparaging their lord and ravaging their people.

"Master Tseng[9] said: *Beware! Beware! Whatever you give out is given back*. It was only now that the people had a chance to give back what you'd given them. You mustn't blame them. If you governed with Humanity, the people would love your officers and die willingly to protect them."

13 Duke Wen of T'eng said: "T'eng is a small nation wedged in between two powerful neighbors. Should I pay court to Ch'i or Ch'u?"

"This kind of thing is beyond me," replied Mencius. "But if you need an answer, I have one suggestion: make your moats deeper and your city walls stronger, then stand beside your people to defend your land. If they would rather die than desert you, your country will be safe."

14 Duke Wen of T'eng said: "The Ch'i army is fortifying Hsüeh. I'm terribly worried. What shall I do?"

"In ancient times," replied Mencius, "Emperor T'ai lived in Pin. But the Ti tribes kept attacking, so he went to settle below Ch'i Mountain.[10] It wasn't something he wanted: he had no choice. If your actions are noble, true emperors will rise again among the children and grandchildren of future generations. Your own success depends upon Heaven alone, but whatever you make and hand down – that will continue.

"What can you possibly do about Ch'i? Just devote yourself to noble actions, and let come what will."

15 Duke Wen of T'eng said: "T'eng is a small nation. We'll run ourselves into the ground paying these great neighbors homage, and still never escape them. What shall I do?"

"In ancient times," replied Mencius, "Emperor T'ai lived in Pin. But the Ti tribes kept attacking. He paid them homage with furs and silks but didn't escape them. He paid them homage with horses and hounds but didn't escape them. He paid them homage with pearls and jade but still didn't escape them. Finally, he called the elders together and said: *What the Ti want is my land. I have heard that the noble-minded will not use what nurtures the people to harm the people. Living without a ruler seems innocuous enough, my friends, so I've decided to leave you.* Setting out from Pin, he crossed the Liang Mountains, founded a new capital below Ch'i Mountain, and there he settled.

"*What Humanity!* cried out the people of Pin. *We can't lose him!*

"Some people followed him like crowds flocking to market. Others said: *This is the land our ancestors watched over. It isn't a question of what we want. We may die defending it, but we can't abandon this land.*

"Choose between these two ways, and you will choose well."

16 Duke P'ing of Lu was about to leave the palace when a trusted advisor named Tsang Ts'ang said: "When you leave you always tell your officials where you're going, my Lord. But now your horses are harnessed and your carriage ready, and you haven't told anyone where you're going. May I ask?"

"I'm going to see Mencius."

"Incredible!" exclaimed Tsang. "How could you debase yourself by going to visit such a commoner, my Lord? Is it because you think he's a sage? A sage is the source of Ritual and Duty. But this Mencius gave his mother a more lavish funeral than his father. You mustn't go see him."

"Yes, perhaps you're right."

Later, Adept Yüeh Cheng entered and said: "Why haven't you gone to see Mencius, my Lord?"

"Because someone told me that Mencius gave his mother a more lavish funeral than his father," replied the duke.

"Incredible! Why do you say it was more lavish? Is it because he mourned his father as a scholar should and mourned his mother as a state minister should? Is it because he made offerings in three vessels for his father and in five for his mother?"

"No, I was thinking about the beauty of his mother's coffin and shroud."

"But it isn't that one was more lavish than the other," said Yüeh Cheng. "He just had more money when his mother died."

Later, Yüeh Cheng went to see Mencius and said: "I told Duke P'ing about you, and he was going to come see you. But the duke has a trusted advisor named Tsang Ts'ang, and he talked him out of it."

"If we go, it's because something urges us on," commented Mencius. "And if we stay, it's because something holds us back. Going and staying – even these are matters beyond our control. It was Heaven that kept me from meeting the duke. This child of the Tsang family – how could he have done such a thing?"

III

1 Kung-sun Ch'ou[1] said: "If you took charge in Ch'i, could you re-create the successes of Kuan Chung[2] and Lord Yen?"

"You certainly are a man of Ch'i," replied Mencius. "You think of no one but Kuan Chung and Lord Yen.

"Someone once asked Tseng Hsi: *Who is the wiser, you or Adept Lu?*

"Tseng Hsi shifted around uneasily and replied: *My father was Master Tseng, and even he was in awe of Lu.*

"Well then, who is the wiser, you or Kuan Chung?

"Tseng's face flushed with anger, and he said: *How could you compare me with Kuan Chung? His sovereign trusted him so utterly, and he ran the government for so long – but his achievements were still utterly meager. How could you compare me with him?*

"If even Tseng Hsi bridled at the idea of being another Kuan Chung, how could you suggest that I would want such a thing?"

"But Kuan Chung made his sovereign the finest of august lords," said Kung-sun, "and Lord Yen led his to such splendor. Are such achievements not worthy of your aspirations?"

"To be a true emperor in Ch'i," replied Mencius, "that would be a simple matter – no harder than turning your hand over."

"Then I'm more confused than ever," said Kung-sun. "Emperor Wen's Integrity was unsurpassed, and he lived to be a hundred, but he still couldn't spread his tranquil rule to all beneath Heaven. His practices were carried on by Emperor Wu and Duke Chou,[3] and only then did great success come. You act like becoming a true emperor is a simple matter – so is Emperor Wen not a worthy exemplar?"

"How could anyone compare to Emperor Wen?" said Mencius. "In the Shang Dynasty, there were six or seven sage emperors between T'ang and Wu Ting, so all beneath Heaven lived content for a long time. And it's hard to change something that's gone on for so long.

"The august lords all paid court to Wu Ting, and so he commanded all beneath Heaven as if he were turning it in the palm of his hand. Chou was a tyrant, but his rule didn't come that much later than Wu Ting's. The traditions of ancient families had been handed down, the ways of good government had been preserved, and he had counselors of great wisdom: Lord Wei, Wei Chung, Prince Pi Kan, Lord Chi, Chiao Ko. That's why he lasted so long before losing everything to Wen. There wasn't a foot of land that wasn't his territory, or a single person who wasn't his subject.

Emperor Wen had such difficulty because he began with only a hundred square miles. The Ch'i people have a saying:

> *Though you may have deep wisdom,*
> *seizing an opportunity works better.*
> *Though you may have a fine hoe,*
> *awaiting the season works better.*

"So in our time, to be a true emperor in Ch'i would be a simple matter. The Hsia, Shang, and Chou never controlled more than a thousand square miles, even at their height – so Ch'i has enough territory. You can hear roosters crowing and dogs barking all the way out to the four borderlands – so Ch'i has enough people. It isn't a question of land or people: to be a true emperor here in Ch'i, all you need is Humane government. Then no one could oppose you.

"But the failures of the emperor have never been greater than they are today, and the sufferings of people under tyranny have never been worse than they are today. It's so easy giving food to the hungry, so easy giving water to the thirsty.

"Confucius said: *Integrity spreads through the land faster than a proclamation sent racing down the line of postal stations*. If a nation of ten thousand war-chariots embraced Humane government today, the people would rejoice as if they'd escaped hanging by their heels. In times like these, you can do half as much as the ancients and get twice the results."

2 Kung-sun Ch'ou said: "Suppose you became prime minister in Ch'i and put the Way into practice, making the Ch'i sovereign an emperor without peer – would you feel moved, or not?"

"My mind[4] has been utterly still since I was forty," replied Mencius.

"Then you must be way beyond Meng Pin."[5]

"That wouldn't be hard. Now Master Kao[6] – he'd stilled his mind even before me."

"Is there a Way to follow in stilling the mind?"

"There is," replied Mencius. "To cultivate great valor, Po-kung Yu never bowed down and never broke off a stare. He knew that the least intimidation was as bad as being slapped in the marketplace. An affront was the same to him whether it came from a peasant or a sovereign who commanded a nation of ten thousand war-chariots, and he'd run his sword through the august lord as easily as the peasant. He knew every insult had to be returned in kind.

"Of cultivating valor, Meng Shih-she said: *I consider defeat victory. To gauge an enemy before attacking, to calculate your chances of success before fighting – that is to live in fear of great armies. How can I ever be certain of victory? All I can do is live without fear.*

"Meng Shih-she was like Master Tseng, and Po-kung Yu

was like Adept Hsia. It's impossible to say which of the two had the most profound valor, but Meng Shih-she nurtured his *ch'i*.[7]

"Long ago, Master Tseng said to Adept Hsiang: *Do you love valor? I once heard about great valor from Confucius. If you look within and find yourself less than honorable, you'll fear even a peasant as an enemy. But if you look within and find yourself honorable, you'll face even an army of ten million men.*

"Meng Shih-she nurtured *ch'i*, but that's still nothing like Master Tseng nurturing essentials."

"May I ask about the stillness of your mind, and the stillness of Master Kao's mind?" asked Kung-sun Ch'ou.

"Master Kao says *Don't search the mind for what you can't find in words, and don't search* ch'i *for what you can't find in the mind,*" replied Mencius. "Not searching *ch'i* for what you can't find in the mind – that's fine. But not searching the mind for what you can't find in words – that isn't.

"The will guides *ch'i*, and *ch'i* fills the body. So for us the will comes first, and ch'i second. That's why I say: *Keep a firm grasp on your will, but never tyrannize your ch'i.*"

At this, Kung-sun Ch'ou said: "If you say *For us the will comes first, and ch'i second,* how can you also say *Keep a firm grasp on your will, but never tyrannize your ch'i?*"

"When the will is whole, it moves *ch'i*, and when *ch'i* is whole, it moves the will. When we stumble and hurry, *ch'i* is affected, but that in turn moves the mind."

"May I ask what makes you excel and flourish so?"

"I understand words, and I nurture the *ch'i*-flood."

"May I ask what you mean by *ch'i*-flood?"

"That's hard to explain," replied Mencius. "It's *ch'i* at its limits: vast and relentless. Nourish it with fidelity and allow it no injury – then it fills the space between Heaven and earth. It is the *ch'i* that unifies Duty and the Way. Without it, we starve. And it's born from a lifetime of Duty: a few token acts aren't enough. When the things we do don't satisfy the mind, we starve.

"That's why I say: *Master Kao still doesn't understand Duty. He thinks it's something outside of us.* You must devote yourself to this *ch'i*-flood without forcing it. Don't let it out of your mind, but don't try to help it grow and flourish either.

"If you do, you'll be acting like that man from Sung who worried that his rice shoots weren't growing fast enough, and so went around pulling at them. At the end of the day, he returned home exhausted and said to his family: *I'm worn out. I've been helping the rice grow.* His son ran out to look and found the fields all withered and dying.

"In all beneath Heaven, there are few who can resist helping the rice shoots grow. Some think nothing they do will help, so they ignore them. They are the ones who don't even bother to weed. Some try to help them grow: they are the ones who pull at them. It isn't just that they aren't making things better – they're actually making them worse!"

"What do you mean by *understanding words*?" asked Kung-sun Ch'ou.

"I understand what lies hidden beneath beguiling words. I understand the trap beneath extravagant words. I understand the deceit beneath depraved words. And I understand the weariness beneath evasive words.

"Born of the mind, such things cripple government. And then what is born of government cripples all our endeavors. If ever great sages arise again, they will confirm what I've said.

"Tsai Yü and Adept Kung were masters of eloquence," said Kung-sun Ch'ou. "Jan Po-niu, Min Tzu-ch'ien, and Yen Hui[8] were masters of Integrity's principles. Confucius had mastered both, and still he said: *I'm not much good at eloquence.* So you must already be a great sage, Master."

"What a thing to say!" responded Mencius. "Long ago, Adept Kung asked Confucius: *And are you a great sage, Master?*

"I couldn't make such a claim, replied Confucius. *I learn relentlessly and teach relentlessly, that's all.*

"At this, Adept Kung said: *To learn relentlessly is wisdom, and to teach relentlessly is Humanity. To master wisdom and Humanity – isn't that to be a sage?*

"So even Confucius couldn't claim to be a sage. What a thing to say!"

"Of those times," said Kung-sun, "I have heard that Adept Hsia, Adept Yu, and Adept Chang each embodied one aspect of the sage completely. And that Jan Po-niu, Min Tzu-ch'ien, and Yen Hui each embodied all aspects of the sage, but only partially. Which of these is preferable?"

"Let's skip that for now."

"What do you think of Po Yi[9] and Yi Yin[10]?"

"Their Ways were different," replied Mencius. "Po Yi refused to serve a sovereign he disdained or govern a people he disdained. So he took office in times of wise rule and renounced office in times of chaos. Yi Yin, on the other hand, thought any sovereign he served was that much more worthy, and any people he served was that much more worthy. So he took office in times of wise rule, and he took office in times of chaos.

"But Confucius was different. If it was wise to take office, he took office; and if it was wise to stay somewhere, he stayed. If it was wise to linger, he lingered; and if it was wise to hurry away, he hurried away.

"All three were great sages of long ago. I cannot compare to any of them. But Confucius is the one I take for a teacher."

"Did Po Yi and Yi Yin so nearly equal Confucius?"

"No. In all the time since people first came into being, there's never been another like Confucius."

"But were they alike in any way?"

"Yes," replied Mencius. "Given a hundred square miles of territory to rule, they could have inspired the august lords to pay them homage and so made all beneath Heaven their own. But if making all beneath Heaven their own meant violating their Duty even once or killing even a single innocent person, they all would have refused. In this they were alike."

"May I ask how they differed?"

"Tsai Yü, Adept Kung, and Master Yu were all wise enough to understand a sage. And they would never defile themselves by giving someone they admired undue praise. Still, Tsai Yü said: *In my view, the Master was a far greater sage than Yao or Shun.*[11]

"Adept Kung said: *Seeing a state's Ritual, he understood its government. And hearing a state's music, he understood its ruler's Integrity. Looking back, he could gauge all the emperors of a hundred generations. And no one ever proved him wrong. In all the time since people first came into being, there's never been another like him.*

"And Master Yu said: *And why only people? Unicorns are like other animals, phoenixes like other birds, T'ai Mountain like com-*

mon hills, rivers and seas like flowing ditches. And the sage is like other people, though he's also different from them: he stands above them. In all the time since people first came into being, there's never been another with the abounding excellence of Confucius."

3 Mencius said: "To pretend force is Humanity – that's the mark of a tyrant, and a tyrant needs a large country. To practice Humanity through Integrity – that's the mark of a true emperor, and a true emperor doesn't need a large country. T'ang began with only seventy square miles, and Emperor Wen began with only a hundred square miles. If you use force to gain the people's submission, it isn't a submission of the heart. It's only a submission of the weak to the strong. But if you use Integrity to gain the people's submission, it's a submission of the sincere and delighted heart. It's like the submission of seventy disciples to Confucius.

"The *Songs* say:

From west and from east,
from south and from north –
every thought in submission.

That says it exactly."

4 Mencius said: "From Humanity comes honor. From Inhumanity comes disgrace. To despise disgrace and yet practice Inhumanity – that's like despising water and living in bottomlands. If you despise disgrace, there's nothing like treasuring Integrity and honoring noble officials. When those of great wisdom are ministers and those of great ability are officials, the nation is untroubled. And if the ruler uses such times of peace to clarify his policies, then even the largest countries will stand in awe of him.

"The *Songs* say:

> *Before the Heavens darkened with rain,*
> *I gathered up mulberry roots,*
> *wove tight window and door.*
> *Now those people down below –*
> *how could they disparage me?*[12]

Whoever wrote this poem certainly understood the Way, commented Confucius. *If a ruler can govern his nation well, how could anyone disparage him?*

"These days, rulers use times of peace to indulge in the pleasures of music and idle amusement. They're bringing ruin down upon themselves. We bring it all upon ourselves: prosperity and ruin alike. The *Songs* say:

> *Always worthy of Heaven's Mandate,*
> *he found great prosperity in himself.*

And the "T'ai Chia"[13] says:

Ruin from Heaven
we can weather.
Ruin from ourselves
we never survive.

That says it exactly."

5 Mencius said: "Honor the wise, employ the able, and you'll have great worthies for ministers – then every noble official throughout all beneath Heaven will rejoice and long to stand in your court. Collect rent in the markets but no tax, or enforce laws but collect no rent – then every merchant throughout all beneath Heaven will rejoice and long to trade in your markets. Conduct inspections at the border but collect no tax – then every traveler throughout all beneath Heaven will rejoice and long to travel your roads. Have farmers help with public fields but collect no tax – then every farmer in all beneath Heaven will rejoice and long to work your land. Don't demand tributes in cloth from families and villages – then people throughout all beneath Heaven will rejoice and long to become your subjects.

"If you can do these five things with sincerity, the people in neighboring countries will all revere you as their parent. And not since people first came into being has anyone ever managed to lead children against their own parents. So if you do this, you won't have an enemy anywhere in all beneath Heaven. When you haven't an enemy anywhere in all beneath Heaven, you'll be Heaven's minister. And no one has become that without becoming a true emperor."

6 Mencius said: "Everyone has a heart that can't bear to see others suffer. The ancient emperors had hearts that couldn't bear to see others suffer, and so had governments that couldn't bear to see others suffer. If you lead a government that can't bear to see others suffer, ruling all beneath Heaven is like turning it in the palm of your hand.

"Suddenly seeing a baby about to fall into a well, anyone would be heart-stricken with pity: heart-stricken not because they wanted to curry favor with the baby's parents, not because they wanted the praise of neighbors and friends, and not because they hated the baby's cries. This is why I say everyone has a heart that can't bear to see others suffer.

"And from this we can see that without a heart of compassion we aren't human, without a heart of conscience we aren't human, without a heart of courtesy we aren't human, and without a heart of right and wrong we aren't human. A heart of compassion is the seed of Humanity. A heart of conscience is the seed of Duty. A heart of courtesy is the seed of Ritual. And a heart of right and wrong is the seed of wisdom.

"These four seeds are as much a part of us as our four limbs. To possess them and yet deny their potential – that is to wound yourself. And to deny the sovereign's potential – that is to wound the sovereign. We all possess these four seeds, and if we all understand how to nurture them, it will be like fire blazing forth or springs flooding free. Nurtured, they're enough to watch over all within the four seas. Unnurtured, they aren't enough to serve even our own parents."

7 Mencius said: "How can the arrow-maker be any less Humane than the armor-maker? It's just that the arrow-maker hopes to wound people and the armor-maker hopes to protect them. It's like this for shaman-healers and coffin-makers too. So you can't be too careful in choosing your trade.

"Confucius said: *Of villages, Humanity is the most beautiful. If you choose to dwell anywhere else – how can you be called wise?*

Humanity is the noble honor Heaven affirms and the tranquil place humans dwell. Failing to practice Humanity when there's nothing stopping you – that is a failure of wisdom. Without Humanity and wisdom, Ritual and Duty, we're nothing but slaves. A slave ashamed of being a slave – that's like a bow-maker ashamed of making bows or an arrow-maker ashamed of making arrows. If you feel shame, there's nothing like practicing Humanity.

"The Humane are like archers. They square up their stance before shooting. And if they fail to hit the mark, they don't resent the victor who does. Instead, they always look within themselves to find the reason for their failure."

8 Mencius said: "Whenever someone told Adept Lu he'd made a mistake, he was delighted. Whenever Emperor Yü heard someone say something honorable, he bowed. But the great Shun – he went way beyond that. Thinking the honorable was something everyone shared, he gave up his own ways and followed the people. He was always happy to adopt what the people considered honorable. From his life as a farmer, potter, and fisherman to his life as emperor, there was nothing he didn't learn by adopting it from the people. And to adopt what the people con-

sider honorable is to help them live honorably. So for the noble-minded, nothing is more important than helping the people live honorably."

9 Mencius said: "Po Yi never served a sovereign he disdained, nor did he remain friends with a friend he disdained. He never served in a foul man's court, or even talked with such a man. Serving such a man or even talking with him – for Po Yi, that was like donning fine court robes to sit in mud and ash. He pushed his hatred of the foul impossibly far: if he met a neighbor whose hat wasn't on straight, he would hurry away without looking back, as if it would tarnish him. That's why he refused all offers from august lords, however honorable the offers were. He refused because it was demeaning to attend them.

"Liu-hsia Hui,[14] on the other hand, wasn't shamed by defiled rulers, nor did he consider common positions below him. When in office, he never hid his wisdom and always depended on the Way. When dismissed, he bore no resentment. And suffering adversity, he remained untroubled. He said: *You are who you are, and I am who I am. Even if you stripped naked and stood beside me, how could you ever tarnish me?* Hence he was completely at ease no matter who he was with, and never insisted on leaving. If he was asked to stay, he stayed – for he never felt demeaned and forced to leave.

"Po Yi was too pinched and Liu-hsia Hui too undignified," commented Mencius. "Pinched and undignified: the noble-minded avoid both."

IV

1 Mencius said: "The seasons of Heaven cannot rival the industry of earth. And the industry of earth cannot rival an accord of the people.

"Suppose there were a city with a three-mile inner wall and a seven-mile outer wall. An army surrounds the city and attacks, but fails to conquer it. To surround the city in the first place, this army must have been blessed by the seasons of Heaven. But it failed to conquer the city because the seasons of Heaven cannot rival the industry of earth.

"Now suppose a city's walls are high, its moat deep, its weapons strong and sharp, its supplies plentiful. But this time, the people abandon it and flee. The city falls because the industry of earth cannot rival an accord of the people.

"And so it is said: *Borders and frontiers can't corral the people. Ranges of mountains can't secure a nation. And sharp weapons can't keep all beneath Heaven in awe.*

"Master the Way and your supporters are countless. Lose the Way and your supporters are few. When your supporters are few, even your own family will turn against you. When you supporters are countless, all beneath Heaven will follow you. Hence, the noble-minded ruler never goes to war, or if he does, victory is a simple matter – for he is followed by all beneath Heaven while his enemy's own family is turning against him."

2 Just as Mencius was about to leave for court, a courier arrived with a message from the emperor: "I wanted to come visit you today, but I have a cold and must avoid the wind. I'll hold court again tomorrow, and wonder if I'll have a chance to see you then?"

To this, Mencius replied: "Unfortunately, I too am sick and so cannot attend court."

The next morning, Mencius went to offer the Tung-kuo family his condolences, whereupon Kung-sun Ch'ou said: "Yesterday you declined the emperor's summons, saying you were sick. But today you're out visiting, offering condolences. Should you really be doing this?"

"Yesterday I was sick," replied Mencius, "but today I am well again. So why shouldn't I go out to offer my condolences?"

The emperor sent someone to see how Mencius was feeling, and a doctor came too. Adept Meng Chung told them: "Yesterday, when the emperor's message arrived, Mencius was sick and could not attend court. Today he's feeling a little better, so he hurried off to court. But I don't know if he'll be able to get there or not."

Meng then sent some people to find Mencius and tell him: "You mustn't return home. Go to the emperor's court at once."

But Mencius still didn't go. Instead, he spent the night at Ching Ch'ou's house. There, Lord Ching said: "Inside the home, there is father and son. Outside, there is sovereign and subject. These are the great bonds of human community. Between father and son, affection rules. Between sovereign and subject, reverence rules. I've seen the emperor's reverence for you, but I have yet to see any sign of your reverence for the emperor."

"What a thing to say!" responded Mencius. "In all of Ch'i, there's no one who talks to the emperor about Humanity and Duty. Is that because they don't consider Humanity and Duty to be beautiful things? Or is it because they say to themselves: *Talking to a person like that about Humanity and Duty – what good would it do?* Is anything more irreverent that that? I've never dared offer the emperor anything less than the Way of Yao and Shun. So is there anyone in all of Ch'i with more reverence for the emperor than I?"

"No," said Lord Ching, "that isn't what I meant. The *Book of Ritual* says: *When your father calls, don't pause to answer.*

When your sovereign summons, don't wait for a carriage. You were leaving for the emperor's court, but when his summons arrived you refused to go. Isn't this a violation of Ritual?"

"So that's what you meant?" replied Mencius. "Master Tseng said: *Nothing can rival the wealth of Chin and Ch'u. Still – they may have wealth, but I have Humanity; and they may have nobility, but I have Duty. So why should I envy them?* If Master Tseng said this, how could it be wrong? It must be part of the one Way.

"There are three things known throughout all beneath Heaven as exalted: nobility, age, and Integrity. At court, nothing rivals nobility. In the village, nothing rivals age. But for nurturing the people, nothing rivals Integrity. How can you ignore two of these because you possess one of them? If a sovereign is doing great things, he must have advisors he cannot summon. If he wants counsel, he goes to them. If he does not honor Integrity and delight in the Way like this, he is not worthy of their help.

"T'ang first took Yi Yin as a teacher, then as a counselor – and so he became a true emperor with ease. Duke Huan first took Kuan Chung as a teacher, then as a counselor – and so he became the finest of august lords with ease.

"Now all beneath Heaven is full of countries equal in territory and Integrity. None can overcome another for one simple reason: their rulers all want advisors they can teach, rather than advisors they can learn from. T'ang never presumed to summon Yi Yin; Duke Huan never presumed to summon Kuan Chung. And Kuan Chung is scarcely worthy of anyone's aspirations. If he was not to be summoned, am I?"

3 Adept Ch'en said: "The Ch'i emperor once offered you a hundred *yi* in the purest gold, and you refused. But now in Sung you've accepted seventy, and in Hsüeh fifty. If your refusal then was right, your acceptance now is wrong. And if your acceptance now is right, your refusal then was wrong. You can only have it one way."

"Both were right," replied Mencius. "In Sung I was leaving on a long journey, and farewell gifts are always given to departing travelers. So when the emperor said *Please accept this farewell gift,* why should I refuse? In Hsüeh I was worried about my safety. The emperor said *I've heard about your worries. This is to help you buy weapons.* So why should I refuse?

"But in Ch'i there was no reason for the gift. A gift for no reason is a bribe. And when have the noble-minded ever taken bribes?"

4 Mencius went to P'ing Lu and said to the governor there: "If you had a spearman who abandoned his post three times in a single day, would you discharge him or not?"

"I wouldn't wait for three times," replied Governor K'ung Chü-hsin.

"But you have abandoned your own post many times," countered Mencius. "In years of calamity and failed harvests, how many thousands of your people suffered – young and old alike abandoned to gutters and ditches, the strong scattered to every corner of the land?"

"But there was nothing I could do."

"Suppose someone entrusted their cattle and sheep to your care. Surely you would try to find grass and hay for them. And if you couldn't find any, would you return them to their owner or just stand by and watch them die?"

"So, I myself am to blame."

Some time later, Mencius went to see the emperor and said: "I know five provincial governors in your country. The only one who understands how he himself is to blame is K'ung Chü-hsin. Shall I tell you what happened?"

"I myself am to blame," replied the emperor.

5 Mencius said to Ch'ih Wa: "When you resigned as governor of Ling Ch'iu and asked to be appointed chief judge, it seemed a wise choice because a chief judge advises the emperor. It's been several months since you were appointed – how is it you still haven't counseled the emperor?"

Soon thereafter, Ch'ih Wa offered his counsel to the emperor. When his counsel was ignored, he resigned and went away.

At this, the Ch'i people said: "What Mencius urged Ch'ih Wa to do was fine indeed. As for what Mencius himself does – things aren't so clear."

When Adept Kung-tu told him about this, Mencius said: "I've heard that officials resign if they cannot fulfill their duties, and that counselors resign if they cannot offer their advice. But I'm neither an official nor a counselor, so when it comes to engagement and withdrawal, why shouldn't I just do as I please?"

6 When Mencius was a minister in Ch'i, he went to T'eng on a mission of condolence. The emperor sent as his deputy Wang Huan, the governor of Ko. But even though Mencius saw Wang Huan morning and night on

their travels to and from T'eng, he never discussed the purpose of their journey.

"The position of minister in Ch'i is no small thing," commented Kung-sun Ch'ou, "and the road between Ch'i and T'eng is hardly short. How is it you traveled all that way and never discussed the purpose of your journey with him?"

"There were others appointed to arrange things," replied Mencius. "What was there for us to discuss?"

7 Mencius traveled from Ch'i to Lu for the burial of his mother. On his way back to Ch'i, he stopped at Ying. There, Ch'ung Yü said: "You didn't think me unworthy of directing the work of the coffin-makers. The work was urgent, so there was no time for questions. But now there's one I'd like to ask, if you don't mind: *Wasn't that awfully beautiful wood?*"

"In the most ancient times, there weren't rules about how coffins were to be built," replied Mencius. "Later on, there were rules requiring inner and outer coffins to be seven inches thick, whether they were for the Son of Heaven or a common peasant. It isn't a question of beauty, but of expressing all that's in our hearts. If we can't find beautiful wood, we feel uneasy. And if we can't afford it, we feel uneasy. So if they could find it, and they could afford to buy it, the ancients always used the most beautiful wood. How could all this be any different for me?

"And to keep soil from the body of a loved one caught in the midst of such a change – is that not a great joy? I've heard that the noble-minded never scrimp when it comes to parents – not for all beneath Heaven."

8 Acting on his own, Shen T'ung[1] asked: "Is an attack against Yen acceptable?"

"Yes," replied Mencius. "Emperor K'uai had no right to abdicate in favor of Lord Chih. And Lord Chih had no right to accept.

"Suppose there was an official that you especially liked, and you gave him your salary and position without telling the emperor. Suppose that he took it without securing the emperor's approval. Would that be acceptable? And how is that any different from what's happened in Yen?"

Soon Ch'i attacked Yen, and someone asked: "Is it true that you encouraged Ch'i to attack Yen?"

"I did not!" bristled Mencius. "When Shen T'ung asked if an attack against Yen would be acceptable, I said *Yes*. And soon Ch'i attacked. But if he'd asked *For whom is an attack against Yen acceptable?* I would have said: *An attack by someone Heaven appointed is acceptable.*

"Suppose one person killed another, and someone asked: *Is the killing of a person acceptable?* I would answer: Yes. But if the question was: *For whom is the killing of a person acceptable?* I would say: *The killing of a person by a chief judge is acceptable.* Now to attack Yen with another Yen – how could I ever encourage such a thing?"

9 The Yen people had turned to rebellion. The Ch'i emperor said: "I'm too ashamed to face Mencius."

"I wouldn't worry too much," said Ch'en Chia.[2] "Who do you consider the most Humane and wise – you or Duke Chou?"

"What a thing to ask!" said the emperor.

"Duke Chou put Kuan Shu in charge of Shang, and then Kuan Shu used Shang to launch his rebellion. If Chou sent Kuan Shu knowing what would happen, he wasn't Humane. And if he sent Kuan Shu without knowing what would happen, he wasn't wise. So Chou's Humanity and wisdom weren't perfect, and how could yours be anything like his? Shall I go explain this to Mencius?"

Ch'en Chia went to see Mencius and asked: "What kind of man was Duke Chou?"

"An ancient sage," replied Mencius.

"Is it true that he put Kuan Shu in charge of Shang, and then Kuan Shu used Shang to launch his rebellion?"

"It is. "

"Did he send Kuan Shu to Shang knowing he would launch a rebellion?"

"No, he didn't know what Kuan Shu was going to do."

"So even a sage makes mistakes?"

"Duke Chou was the younger brother, and Kuan Shu the elder," replied Mencius. "So it's hardly surprising Chou would make such a mistake. But in ancient times, when the noble-minded made mistakes, they knew how to change. These days, when the noble-minded make mistakes, they persevere to the bitter end. In ancient times, mistakes of the noble-minded were like eclipses of sun and moon: there for all the people to see. And when a mistake was made right, the people all looked up in awe. But these days, the noble-minded just persevere to the bitter end, and then they invent all kinds of explanations."

10 Mencius resigned his office and returned home. The emperor went to see him and said: "I wanted to come see you the other day, but could not. When we served together in the same court, I was overjoyed. But now you've

left me and returned to your home. I wonder if I can still come here to see you?"

"I wouldn't have dared ask," replied Mencius, "but that is my deepest wish."

Another day, the emperor said to Lord Shih: "I want to give Mencius a house in the center of the capital and ten thousand measures of rice to support his disciples. Then my ministers and people will always have a noble example there before them. Would you talk to him for me?"

Lord Shih passed this message to Mencius through his disciple, Adept Ch'en. When Ch'en gave Shih's message to him, Mencius said: "I see. Yes, how would Lord Shih know such a thing cannot be done? Perhaps he thinks I'm after wealth. But if I were after wealth, why would I give up a hundred thousand so I could have ten thousand?

"Chi Sun once said: *Adept Shu Yi was strange indeed. He arranged an appointment for himself, and when his counsel was ignored, he resigned. But then he used this to arrange lofty appointments for his sons and brothers. People all want wealth and renown, of course. But there in the midst of it, he certainly found his high ground.*

"In the ancient markets, people simply traded what they had for what they had not. The government supervised, nothing more. But then came an uncivil old man who always searched out high ground and climbed up on top. Surveying the situation carefully, he found all the profits to be had, then snared every one. The people all thought him uncivil, so they taxed him. And so it was that the taxing of merchants began."

11 Mencius left Ch'i and spent the night in Chou. There, on behalf of the Chou emperor, a man wanted to convince Mencius to stay. He sat down and began talking to Mencius, but Mencius said nothing. Instead, he fell asleep with his head on the table. Quite unhappy, the man said: "I fasted a full day and night before daring to speak with you. But instead of listening, you sleep. I won't disturb you again."

"Please sit," said Mencius. "I'll try to explain this clearly. Long ago, if Duke Mu of Lu didn't have someone always by Master Szu's[3] side, Szu soon lost interest in him. On the other hand – if Hsieh Liu and Shen Hsiang didn't have someone always by Duke Mu's side, Mu soon lost interest in them.

"Now you've gone to all this trouble, but I'm certainly not being treated the way Master Szu was. So am I ignoring you, or are you ignoring me?"

12 Talking with some people after Mencius left Ch'i, Yin Shih said: "If he didn't know the emperor would never be another T'ang or Wu, he isn't very bright. If he knew this and came anyway, he was just trying to get ahead. He came a thousand miles to see the emperor, failed, and left disappointed – but then it took him three days to leave Chou. What made him linger there? It all seems rather suspect to me."

When Adept Kao told him about this, Mencius said: "What does Yin Shih know about me? When I came a thousand miles to see the emperor, that was what I wanted. But to fail and leave disappointed – how could that be what I wanted? It was something I couldn't avoid.

"I waited three days to leave Chou, it's true, but even that felt too soon. The emperor was on the verge of a transformation, and if that had happened he would have called me back. Only when I left Chou and the emperor still didn't send after me – only then did the longing for home well up. But had I abandoned the emperor even then?

"The emperor is capable of noble things. If he'd listened to me, it would have meant peace not just for the people of Ch'i, but for the people throughout all beneath Heaven. The emperor was on the verge of a transformation, and every day I hoped for that. So am I like the little man whose face clouds over with anger and resentment when the sovereign ignores his counsel, who leaves and travels hard all day before stopping?"

When Yin Shih heard this, he said: "It is I who am the little man."

13 Mencius left Ch'i. As they traveled away, Ch'ung Yü said: "You look so unhappy, Master. But just the other day I heard you say: *The noble-minded never resent Heaven and never blame people.*"

"That was then," replied Mencius. "This is now. A true emperor should arise every five hundred years, and there should also arise others worthy of renown in their time. It's been over seven hundred years since the Chou began: enough time and more. And surely the world is ready. But it seems Heaven still doesn't want to bring peace and order to all beneath Heaven. If it did, who could it choose in our time besides me? So why should I be unhappy?"

14 Mencius had left Ch'i and was staying in Hsiu. There, Kung-sun Ch'ou asked: "To serve in office but refuse a salary – is that the ancient Way?"

"No," replied Mencius. "I was ready to leave after seeing the Ch'i emperor once. And I wasn't about to change my mind – that's why I refused a salary. But then war broke out, so I couldn't very well ask to leave. I had no intention of staying so long."

V

1 When he was heir apparent, Duke Wen of T'eng went on a journey to Ch'u. He went by way of Sung, and there stopped to see Mencius. Mencius told him that people are inherently good, and that he must strive to equal Yao and Shun.

When he returned from Ch'u, the duke again stopped to see Mencius, and Mencius said: "Do you doubt what I told you? There is one and only one Way. Ch'eng Chien said to Duke Ching of Ch'i: *Those sage-emperors were men, and I am a man. Why should I be in awe of them?* Yen Hui[1] said: *What kind of man was Shun, and what kind of man am I? If we're devoted, we can be like him.* And Kung-ming Yi said: *Emperor Wen is my teacher. And how could he ever deceive me?*

"Now if you evened out the borders, T'eng would measure fifty square miles: big enough to do great things. The *Book of History* says: *If herbs don't make your head swim, they won't cure your illness.*"

2 Wen was heir apparent when Duke Ting of T'eng passed away, so he said to Jan Yu: "Mencius once

counseled me in Sung, and I've never forgotten a word of what he said. The death of a father is a time of great sorrow and responsibility. Before I do anything, I want you to go see Mencius and ask his advice.

Jan Yu went to see Mencius in Chou, and Mencius said: "This is a good thing. Mourning a parent's death – that is when you face yourself utterly. Master Tseng said: *In life, serve parents according to Ritual. In death, bury them according to Ritual. And then make offerings to them according to Ritual. Do this, and you can be called a worthy child.*

"I've never studied the rituals of august lords. Still, I have heard something about such matters. The practice has been the same for three dynasties, and for everyone from the Son of Heaven to simple peasants: a mourning period of three years, clothes of plain cloth cut straight, meals of common porridge."

When Jan Yu returned and reported what Mencius had said, Wen decided to observe a three-year mourning period. But the elders and the hundred officials protested: "This is not the way of the ancestral rulers in Lu, our homeland, nor is it the way of our own ancestral rulers. And to violate their practice – that is not for you to do. The *Annals* say: *In mourning and sacrifice, follow the ways of your ancestors.*"

"My way has also been handed down from the ancients," said Wen.

Later, he said to Jan Yu: "In the past, I spent my time with horses and swords rather than books and teachers. And now the elders and the hundred officials all consider me lacking, so I'm afraid they won't devote themselves to the great issues of our nation. Go for me, and seek the counsel of Mencius."

So Jan Yu returned to Chou and inquired of Mencius.

"I see," replied Mencius. "Why does he look to others for his answers? Confucius said:

> *When the sovereign dies – trust government to the prime minister, drink broth, wear a charcoal face dark as ink. Take your place and mourn, then none of the hundred officials will dare be without grief. Show others the way, for the commitments of leaders become the passions of followers. The noble-minded have the Integrity of wind, and little people the Integrity of grass. When the wind sweeps over grass, it bends.*

So these things depend upon Wen alone."

When Jan Yu returned and reported what Mencius had said, Wen said: "I see. Yes, these things do depend upon me and me alone."

For five months he stayed in his mourning hut, issuing no proclamations or precepts. Soon both the hundred officials and the family could both say: "How wise!" And when it came time for the burial, people traveled from every corner of the land to watch. The sorrow in his face, the grief in his sobs: it was a great comfort to the other mourners.

3 Duke Wen of T'eng asked about governing his country, and Mencius said: "Never neglect the endeavors of the people. The *Songs* say:

> *We gather thatch-reeds by day,*
> *and braid rope into the night.*
> *We hurry to build field huts,*
> *then begin planting the hundred grains.*

This is how the people live: it's their Way.

"With a constant livelihood, people's minds are constant. Without a constant livelihood, people's minds are never constant. And without constant minds, they wander loose and wild. They stop at nothing, and soon cross the law. Then, if you punish them accordingly, you've done nothing but snare the people in your own trap. And if they're Humane, how can those in high position snare their people in traps?

"Therefore, the wise ruler practices humility, economy, and reverence toward his subjects. And he takes from the people only what is due him. Yang Hu said: *If you cultivate wealth, you give up Humanity. If you cultivate Humanity, you give up wealth.*

"In the Hsia Dynasty, each family had fifty acres and paid a personal tax. In the Shang, each family had seventy acres and paid a mutual tax. And in the Chou, each family had a hundred acres and paid a communal tax. But in fact, the people always paid one part in ten. *Communal* means *everyone* together, and *mutual* means *mutual assistance.*[2]

"Master Lung said: *In administering the land, nothing is better than the mutual system, and nothing worse than the personal.* The personal tax is based on harvest averages over a number of years. In good years, when there's a wild abundance of rice and a heavy tax would hardly be noticed, little is taken. But in bad years, when the harvest isn't worth the manure it grew from, the tax is exorbitant. When the people's father and mother wears them out with worry, letting them work desperately all year long and then go into debt just to care for their parents, when he abandons young and old alike to gutters and ditches – how can he be called the people's father and mother?

"As for ensuring a livelihood for descendants of worthy officials, that is already the practice in T'eng. But the *Songs* say:

When rain falls on our public land,
it also falls on our private land.

Only in the mutual system is there public land. These lines are about the Chou, so there's no doubt that it too used the mutual system.

"*Hsiang, hsü, hsüeh,* and *hsiao* were established for the education of the people. *Hsiang* for nurturing, *hsiao* for educating, and *hsü* for archery: these are the names used for village schools. In the Hsia Dynasty they were called *hsiao,* in the Shang *hsü,* and in the Chou *hsiang.* For schools of advanced studies, all three dynasties used the name *hsüeh.* But the purpose of all alike was to illuminate the bonds of human community for the people. And when leaders themselves illuminate those bonds, the common people are full of tender affection. If a true emperor arose, he would have to come learn these things from you, and then you would be the teacher of emperors.

"The *Songs* say:

Chou may be an ancient country,
but its mandate is renewed again.

It was Emperor Wen who renewed it. If you devoted yourself, there's no doubt you could renew your own nation in the same way.

Duke Wen sent Pi Chan to ask about the well-field system,[3] and Mencius said: "Your sovereign is anxious to practice Humane government. He chose carefully when he sent you, so you must spare no effort.

"Humane government begins in settled boundaries. Unless settled boundaries are properly fixed, the well-fields won't be divided equally, nor will the yield given for official salaries be fair. This is why tyrants and corrupt officials always avoid settled boundaries. But once settled boundaries are properly fixed, land shares and salary amounts are easily established.

"T'eng has very little territory. Still, you need both noble-minded leaders and peasants in the countryside. Without noble-minded leaders, who will foster order among the peasants? And without peasants, who will nurture the noble-minded leaders?

"In the countryside, tax people one ninth of their produce, according to the well-field system. In the capital, tax people one tenth of their income. From ministers down, officials should all have fifty acres for sacrificial offerings. And among the peasants, each extra man in a family should be given an additional twenty-five acres. People should never leave their village – not when they move their house and not when they die. If villagers sharing well-fields are friends in all things, help each other keep watch, and care for each other in illness – then the people will live in affection and harmony.

"Each square mile of land contains a well-field, and each well-field contains nine hundred acres. The central plot is public land. The eight families each own a hundred acres of private land, and together they cultivate the public land. Once the public land has been tended, they can turn to their own. This is what distinguishes peasants from officials.

"Such are the broad outlines. As for the details of making all this work well, the refinements and elaborations – that's up to you and your sovereign."

4 There was a man named Hsü Hsing who claimed to follow the Way of Shen Nung.[4] He left Ch'u and journeyed to T'eng, where he went to the palace gate and said to Duke Wen: "I lived in a land far away, and there heard that you practice Humane government. I want to live under your rule, so I've come to ask for a piece of land." The Duke granted Hsü Hsing's request, and Hsü soon had dozens of disciples, all of whom wore sackcloth and earned their living by making sandals and weaving mats.

Ch'en Hsiang and his brother were disciples of Ch'en Liang. Leaving Sung with plows on their backs, they journeyed to T'eng and said: "We have heard that yours is the government of a sage, and we want to live under the rule of a sage."

Ch'en Hsiang went to see Hsü Hsing one day, and was overjoyed. He abandoned his old teacher and took Hsü Hsing as his teacher. He later went to see Mencius and told him what Hsü Hsing had said: "The T'eng sovereign is truly wise and worthy, but he's never learned of the Way. A wise and worthy sovereign earns his living by cultivating the land with his people. It's during breakfast and dinner that he rules. But here, with all his granaries and treasuries, the duke wounds the people while pampering himself. So how can he be wise and worthy?"

"Does Master Hsü eat only the grain he himself has grown?" asked Mencius.

"Yes," replied Ch'en Hsiang.

"And does Master Hsü wear only cloth he himself has woven?"

"No, but he wears only sackcloth."

"Does Master Hsü wear a hat?"

"Yes."

"What kind?"

"Raw silk."

"Did he weave it himself?"

"No, he traded grain for it."

"How is it Master Hsü doesn't weave his own hat?"

"It would interfere with his farm work."

"Does Master Hsü use metal and stoneware for cooking? And for plowing, does he use iron?"

"He does."

"And does he make all these things himself?"

"No, he trades grain for them."

"To trade grain for tools and implements doesn't hurt potters and smithies," said Mencius. "They trade their tools and implements for grain, and does that hurt farmers? Why doesn't Master Hsü become a potter and smithy as well, so he himself can make everything his home needs? The markets of those who practice the hundred crafts are pure bedlam: why does he join in the confusion of barter and trade? How can he bear it?"

"You can't practice a craft and be a farmer too."

"Then how could someone govern all beneath Heaven and also be a farmer? There are the endeavors of great men, and the endeavors of small men. And whatever they need, the hundred crafts provide. If we all had to make things before we could use them, we'd all spend our lives running back and forth on the roads.

"And so it is said:

> *Some use their minds to work, and some use their muscles. Those who use their minds govern, and those who*

> *use their muscles are governed. Those who are governed provide for those who govern, and those who govern are provided for by those who are governed.*

People throughout all beneath Heaven know this to be sound practice.

"In the time of Emperor Yao, things were still wild and unsettled in all beneath Heaven. Rivers burst their banks and floods raged across the world. Grasses and trees grew thick with abandon. Birds and animals roamed everywhere in herds and flocks. The five grains never grew tall. Birds and animals crowded people in: even the Middle Kingdom was a tangle of animal trails and bird tracks.

"It was Yao who worried about how to change all this. He fostered Shun so he could bring order to things. Shun assigned Yi to manage fire, and Yi set fire to the mountains and marshes, sending the birds and animals into hiding. Yü carved out the nine rivers. He cleared the Chi and T'a, and sent them flowing into the sea. He opened up the Ju and Han, banked up the Huai and Szu – and sent them all flowing into the Yangtze. Only then were the people of the Middle Kingdom able to grow food. To do this work, Yü spent eight years away from home and passed by his gate three times without entering. Even if he'd wanted to tend fields, how could he have done it?

"Hou Chi taught the ways of agriculture to the people,

taught them how to plant the five grains. And when the five grains ripened, the people were well fed. But once people have plenty of food and warm clothes, they lead idle lives. This is their Way. Then, unless they're taught, they're hardly different from the birds and animals. The sage-emperor worried about this. He made Hsieh minister of education so the people would be taught about the bonds of human community: affection between father and son, Duty between sovereign and subject, responsibility between husband and wife, proper station between young and old, sincerity between friend and friend.

"Yao said:

> *Encourage them and reward them.*
> *Help them and perfect them.*
> *Support them and give them wings,*
> *and reveal them to themselves.*
> *Then you will bring Integrity alive in them.*

If a sage ruler worries about his people like this, how could he have time for farming? Yao's great worry was that he might not find a Shun. And Shun's great worry was that he might not find a Yü or Kao Yao.[5] If your great worry is tending your own hundred acres, you're simply a farmer.

"To share your wealth is called generosity. To teach people about living nobly is called loyalty. To be worthy of all beneath Heaven is called Humanity – and so it's easy to give all beneath Heaven away, but to be worthy of it is difficult indeed.

"Confucius said:

> *Great indeed was the rule of Yao! Heaven alone is truly majestic, and only Yao could equal it. He was boundless, so vast and boundless the people couldn't even name him. And how majestic, how exalted and majestic a ruler Shun was: possessing all beneath Heaven as if it were nothing to him!*

Ruling all beneath Heaven, didn't Yao and Shun have enough to worry about? How could they worry about farm work too? I've heard of our ways converting barbarians into Chinese, but I've never heard of Chinese reverting into barbarians.

"Ch'en Liang is a product of Ch'u. But he admired the Way of Duke Chou and Confucius, so he came north to study in the Middle Kingdom. Among scholars from the north, none could better him. He could only be called a truly great scholar. You and your brother studied under him for dozens of years. Then he dies and you suddenly turn against him.

"After Confucius died and their three years of mourning were over, his disciples packed their things and prepared to return home. They went in and bowed to Adept Kung. They faced each other and wept until they'd all lost their voices. Only then did they leave for home. Adept Kung returned to the burial grounds, built a hut, and lived alone there for another three years before he finally set out for home.

"Eventually, Adept Hsia, Adept Chang and Adept Yu came to think Master Yu was as wise as the sage, and so wanted to study under him as they had under Confucius. They tried to convince Master Tseng to join them, but Tseng said: *I could never do that. Rinsed clean by the Yangtze and Han rivers, bleached by the autumn sun – something shimmering so perfectly white is beyond compare.*

"Now some tribesman with a twittering shrike's tongue comes from the south condemning the Way of the ancient emperors, and you turn against your teacher and go to study with him. You're nothing like Master Tseng. I've heard of leaving dark ravines to live in high trees, but I've never heard of leaving high trees to live in dark ravines.

"In the *Songs,* among the 'Hymns of Lu,' there's a poem that speaks of

> *fighting down the wild tribes*
> *and punishing Ch'u and Shu.*

Duke Chou fought these people to rescue the Middle Kingdom, and now you want to study under them. Yours was a poor conversion indeed.

"In Master Hsü's Way, market prices should all be the same. He claims that would end deceit, that even if children were sent to market, no one would cheat them. Cloth of the same length would bring the same price, whether it was cotton or silk. Bundled fiber of the same weight would bring the same price, whether it was hemp or silk. The five grains would bring the same price for the same measure, and shoes would all bring the same price for the same size.

"But inequality is the very nature of things. One thing may be two or five times as valuable as another, or perhaps ten or a hundred times, or even a thousand or ten thousand times. If you tried to make everything equal in value, confusion would reign in all beneath Heaven. If elegant shoes and workaday shoes brought the same price, who would bother to make elegant shoes? If we follow the Way of Master Hsü, we'll lead each other into utter deceit. How could a nation be governed this way?"

5 A follower of Mo Tzu[6] named Yi Chih wanted to go see Mencius, so he asked Hsü Pi to arrange a visit. Mencius said: "I would like very much to see him, but I'm quite ill. When I'm feeling better, I'll go see him. He needn't come here."

Later, Yi Chih again tried to arrange a visit with Mencius, and Mencius said: "Now I can see him. But first I must straighten him out a little – for if he isn't thinking straight, how can he see the Way?

"I have heard Adept Yi is a follower of Mo Tzu. In funerals, Mo Tzu's school follows the Way of simplicity. And Adept Yi apparently thinks such simplicity can transform all beneath Heaven. So how can he himself denounce it instead of treasure it? He gave his parents lavish burials, but the principle of simplicity condemns that as a tawdry way of serving them."

When Master Hsü told Adept Yi what Mencius had said, Adept Yi replied: "According to the Confucian Way, the ancients ruled *as if watching over newborn children.* What can such words mean if not that our love should be the same for everyone, even if it always begins with loving our parents?"

When Master Hsü told Mencius what Adept Yi had said, Mencius replied: "Does Adept Yi really believe we can love a neighbor's newborn child the way we love our own brother's child? The only time that's true is when the newborn is crawling around a well and about to fall in, for the child doesn't know any better. Heaven gives birth to all things: they have a single source. But Adept Yi insists they have two, that's why he believes such things.

"Imagine people long ago who didn't bury their parents. When their parents die, they toss them into gullies. Then one day they pass by and see them there: bodies eaten away by foxes and sucked dry by flies. They break into a sweat and can't bear to look. That sweat on their faces isn't a show for their neighbors: it's a reflection of their deepest feelings. So when they go home and return with baskets and shovels to bury their parents, it's because burying parents truly is the right thing, the Way for all worthy children and Humane people."

When Master Hsü told Adept Yi what Mencius had said, Adept Yi grew pensive. Eventually he said: "I have now been taught."

VI

DUKE WEN OF T'ENG *Book Two*

1 Ch'en Tai[1] said: "It seems small of you – refusing to go see the august lords. If you did, you could make whoever you met a true emperor – or at the very least, the finest of august lords. The *Annals* say: *Bend a foot to straighten ten.* It seems worth doing, doesn't it?"

Mencius replied: "Once when he was out hunting, Duke Ching of Ch'i summoned his gamekeeper with a plume-crested flag. The gamekeeper didn't come, so the duke wanted to have him executed, but Confucius said: *A man of great resolve never forgets that he could be abandoned to ditches and gutters, and a man of great valor never forgets that he could lose his head.* What was it Confucius admired in the gamekeeper? The man wasn't entitled to such a lofty summons, so he didn't answer it. And how would it be if people came without waiting for a summons?[2]

"And besides, *bend a foot to straighten ten* is talking about profits. When it's a matter of turning a profit, don't people think it's fine even if they bend ten feet to straighten one?

"Once, because Hsi was a favorite of his, Lord Chien of Chao assigned Wang Liang to drive for him. Hsi didn't catch a single bird all day, so he returned to Lord Chien saying: *He's the worst driver in all beneath Heaven.*

"When someone told him what Hsi had said, Wang Liang said: *Let me try again.* It took no small amount of persuasion, but Hsi finally agreed. This time Hsi caught ten birds in a single morning, and on returning exclaimed: *He's the finest driver in all beneath Heaven!*

"*Then I'll let him drive for you all the time,* said Lord Chien.

"But when he told Wang Liang, Wang Liang refused: *I drove hard for him according to the precepts, and we didn't catch a single bird all day. Then I drove shamelessly for him, and in a single morning we caught ten birds. The* Songs *say:*

> *They drove with flawless skill,*
> *shot arrows with fierce precision.*

I'm not accustomed to driving for little people. I'll go now, if you please.

"Even though he was a mere driver, Wang was ashamed to compromise for an archer. They could have piled birds and animals up like mountains, but he still wouldn't do it. What kind of person would bend the Way to please others? You've got it all wrong: if you bend yourself, you'll never straighten anyone else."

2 Ching Ch'un[3] said: "How could Kung-sun Yen and Chang Yi[4] be anything less than truly great men? If their anger flashed, the august lords cowered. And if they were content, all beneath Heaven was tranquil."

"Does that make them great men?" replied Mencius. "Haven't you studied Ritual? When a boy comes of age, he receives his father's mandate. When a girl marries, she receives her mother's mandate. Saying farewell at the gate, she cautions her: *Now that you're going to your new home, you must be reverent and cautious, and never disobey your husband.* To make deference the norm – that is the Way of married women.

"As for the man who can be called great: He dwells in the most boundless dwelling-place[5] of all beneath Heaven, places himself at the center of all beneath Heaven, and practices the great Way of all beneath Heaven. If he succeeds in these ambitions, he and the people enjoy the rewards together. If he fails, he follows the Way alone. Wealth and renown never mean much to him, poverty and obscurity never sway him, and imposing force never awes him."

3 Chou Hsiao asked: "In ancient times, did the noble-minded take office?"

"They did," replied Mencius. "The *Chronicles* say: *When Confucius went three months without a position, he got anxious and restless. And when he left one nation for another, he always carried his token of credentials with him.*[6]

"And Kung-ming Yi said: *When the ancients went three months without a position, people began offering condolences.*

"Offering condolences after three months!" responded Chou Hsiao. "Is it really all that urgent?"

"When a man loses his office," replied Mencius, "it's like an august lord losing his nation. The *Book of Ritual* says:

> *An august lord helps plow and plant to provide sacrificial grains. His wife helps spin silk to make sacrificial clothes. If the animals are not fat, the grains not clean, the garments not ready, he dare not perform the sacrifice.*
>
> *And if an official holds no land, he performs no sacrifice. If the sacrificial animals, ritual vessels, and sacrificial garments are not all ready, he dare not perform the sacrifice or offer a banquet.*

Isn't that reason enough for condolences?"

"Why is it Confucius always carried his token of credentials with him when he left one nation for another?" asked Chou Hsiao.

"An official serving in office is like a farmer working the

land. If a farmer left one nation for another, would he leave his plow behind?"

"People serve government here in Chin, too," said Chou Hsiao, "but I've never heard of such urgency. If taking office is such an urgent thing, why is it such a difficult question for the noble-minded?"

"When a son is born, parents hope he will one day have a home and family. When a daughter is born, they hope she will one day find a husband. Parents all feel this way. But if children don't wait for their parents' blessings or the arrangements of a matchmaker, if they drill holes in the wall to peer at each other or climb over it for secret meetings, their parents and everyone else think it's appalling.

"Worthy ancients all wanted to serve in office, but never if it meant violating the Way. To secure a position by violating the Way – is that any different from drilling a hole in a wall?"

4 P'eng Keng[7] said: "Traveling around, preaching to august lords for your rice, scores of carriages and hundreds of followers trailed out behind you – isn't that awfully indulgent?"

"If what you do for someone violates the Way," replied Mencius, "accepting even a basketful of rice from them is too much. But abiding in the Way, Shun accepted all beneath Heaven from Yao and didn't think it indulgent. But perhaps you would call it indulgent?"

"No," replied P'eng Keng. "But still, it's shameful when a man doesn't work to earn his rice."

"If someone like you won't trade what you have for what you need, farmers will be left with useless grain and women with useless cloth. But if you will, carpenters and carriage-makers can earn their rice from you. Now here's a man who is a worthy child at home and humble when away, who learned the Way of ancient emperors, preserving it for future students – and you don't think he's even worth feeding. How can you honor carpenters and carriage-makers, but not a master of Humanity and Duty?"

"When carpenters and carriage-makers work, their motive is rice," replied P'eng Keng. "But when the noble-minded practice the Way – is their motive nothing more than rice?"

"Why are you talking about motives?" countered Mencius. "When someone works for you, he deserves to be fed and should be. And besides, do you feed people for their motives or their work?"

"For their motives."

"So if there's a man flinging mortar around and smashing tiles, and his motive is rice, do you feed him?"

"No."

"Then you don't feed people for their motives; you feed them for their work."

5 Wan Chang[8] said: "Sung is a small nation. If its government became that of a true emperor and it were therefore invaded by Ch'i and Ch'u, what could be done?"

"When T'ang lived in Po," replied Mencius, "Po bordered on Ko, which had a ruler who was dissolute and neglected the sacrifices. When T'ang sent someone to ask why the sacrifices were being neglected, Ko's ruler said: *We don't have enough animals.* T'ang sent him cattle and sheep, but instead of using them for sacrifices, he used them for food.

"Again T'ang sent someone to ask why the sacrifices were being neglected, and the Ko ruler said: *We don't have enough millet.* So T'ang sent Po people to help plow and plant, he sent gifts of food for the old and young. But the Ko ruler ambushed them: he led his people out to steal their wine and food, millet and rice. Anyone who resisted was killed: even a boy bringing millet and meat was killed and his gifts stolen.

"The *Book of History* speaks of this: *For the ruler of Ko, the bearers of gifts were enemies.* And when T'ang sent an army to avenge the murder of this boy, everyone within the four seas said: *It isn't lust for all beneath Heaven: it's revenge for the abuse of common men and women.*

"Emperor T'ang began his expeditions in Ko, says the *Book of History.* After eleven expeditions, he hadn't an enemy left anywhere in all beneath Heaven. When he marched east, the western tribes complained. And when he marched south, the northern tribes complained: *Why does he leave us for last?* People watched for him the way they watched for rain in the midst of a great drought. When he came, they went to market unhindered again and weeded their fields without interference. He punished the rulers and comforted the people, like rain falling in its season. And so a great joy rose among the people. The *Book of History* says: *We're waiting for our lord: his coming will end our suffering.*

"It also says:

> *When Yu refused to submit, Emperor Wu marched east and soothed its men and women. They filled baskets with azure-Heaven silk and yellow-earth silk. They went to Wu saying: 'Let us rest here before you. We will cleave to the state of Chou and serve it alone.'*

The noble-minded of Yu offered baskets of Heaven-and-earth silk to welcome the noble-minded of Chou. The peasants of Yu offered baskets of food and jars of wine to welcome the peasants of Chou. Emperor Wu rescued the people from fire and flood, seizing only their cruel rulers.

"In "The Great Declaration," Wu says:

> *Let us brandish weapons and strength.*
> *Let us strike deep into their homelands,*
> *and seizing the tyrants ruling there,*
> *put them to death for everyone to see.*
> *Then our splendor will outshine T'ang's.*

If Sung doesn't have the government of a true emperor, it could fall like that. But if it does have the government of a true emperor, everyone within the four seas will raise their heads and watch for him, wanting him for their sovereign. Then, even though Ch'i and Ch'u are large and powerful nations, what would he have to fear from them?"

6 Mencius said to Tai Pu-sheng: "You wish your emperor were noble and worthy? I'll try to explain this clearly. Suppose a high minister of Ch'u wanted his son to learn the language of Ch'i. Should he get someone from Ch'i to teach his son, or someone from Ch'u?"

"Someone from Ch'i."

"With only a single teacher from Ch'i and everyone else around the boy yammering in Ch'u, the father could cane him every day and he'd still never speak Ch'i. But if he took his son to some district in Ch'i for a few years, then he could cane the boy every day and he'd never speak Ch'u.

"Now, because you consider Hsüeh Chü-chou a noble and worthy man, you've appointed him to serve among the emperor's closest advisors. If among these advisors old and young, stately and humble, there were only men like Hsüeh Chü-chou – who could help the emperor commit ignoble acts? And if among these advisors old and young, stately and humble, there were none like Hsüeh Chü-chou – who would help him act nobly? One Hsüeh Chü-chou, alone – what can he do for the Sung emperor?"

7 Kung-sun Ch'ou asked: "Never trying to see august lords and advise them: is that a form of Duty?"

"In ancient times, if you didn't hold office you didn't see the sovereign," replied Mencius. "Tuan-kan Mu fled over a wall to avoid his sovereign, and Hsieh Liu bolted the door so his couldn't get in. But they were fanatics. When rulers show such determination, it's all right to see them.

"Yang Hu wanted to see Confucius, and yet wasn't willing to compromise Ritual propriety. But the custom is: if a scholar is not at home to receive a high minister's gift, he goes to the minister's gate and bows in thanks. So Yang Hu waited for Confucius to go out, then sent him a steamed piglet. Confucius likewise waited for Yang Hu to go out, then went to his house and bowed before the gate. If Yang Hu had simply asked to see him, how could Confucius have refused?

"Master Tseng said: *Shrugging shoulders and forcing smiles – it's more grueling than hot summer fieldwork.*

"Adept Lu replied: *To say you agree when you don't, and pretend blushing keeps you honest – I can't understand that at all.*

"From this it's easy to understand what the noble-minded cultivate in themselves."

8 Tai Ying-chih said: "To levy only a ten percent tax on income, to abolish all other taxes, including those at the borders and in the markets – that isn't something we can do this year. What if we reduce these taxes now, and give them up completely next year?"

"Suppose someone stole one of his neighbor's chickens every day," replied Mencius. "Suppose someone said to him *This is not the noble-minded Way,* and he replied *What if I only steal one a month for now, and give it up completely next year?*

"If you recognize something is wrong, you want to see it end quickly. So how can you wait until next year?"

9 Adept Kung-tu said: "Everyone but your own disciples thinks you love to argue, Master. Is it true?"

"It isn't that I love to argue," replied Mencius. "I just can't see how to avoid it. All beneath Heaven has endured for ages and ages – sometimes in peace, sometimes in confusion. In the time of Emperor Yao, floods raged across the Middle Kingdom. Snakes and dragons filled the land, leaving nowhere for the people to settle. Lowland people built nests in the treetops; highland people camped in caves.

"The *Book of History* says: *The flood was a warning to us.* And the flood was nothing less than a vast deluge, so Yao appointed Yü to bring the waters under control. Yü dug furrows in the land and sent the waters flowing into the sea. He drove the snakes and dragons into marshes. Where the water rushed toward the sea, it carved out rivers: the Yangtze and Huai, the Yellow and Han. Obstacles and dangers were rinsed away, and ravaging birds and animals disappeared. Only then could people level farmland and settle down.

"But once Yao and Shun died, the Way of sages began to unravel. One savage ruler followed another. They leveled houses to build their pleasure lakes, leaving the people without a place to rest. They let the fields go wild, turning them into parks and preserves, leaving the people without silk and rice. Twisty words and savage acts became official policy. And with the spread of parks and preserves, ponds and lakes, swarms of birds and animals soon returned. By the time of Tyrant Chou, all beneath Heaven was pure chaos. Duke Chou helped Emperor Wu put an end to Tyrant Chou. He conquered Yen after a three-year war and executed its ruler. He drove Fei Lien to the edge of the sea and there put him to death. He conquered fifty nations, drove away all the tigers and leopards, rhinos and elephants. And so, a great joy rose throughout all beneath Heaven. The *Book of History* says:

> *How vast the splendor of Emperor Wen's plans*
> *and the glory of Emperor Wu fulfilling them:*
> *preserving and inspiring us who come later,*
> *they were perfectly true and without flaw.*

"But after them, things began to unravel again, and the Way grew weak. Twisty words and savage acts again became official policy. There were ministers killing emperors, and sons killing fathers. Confucius was heartsick, so he wrote *The Spring and Autumn Annals.* It talks about issues the Son of Heaven faces, which is why Confucius said: *If people understand me, it's because of* The Spring and Autumn Annals; *and if they condemn me, it's also because of* The Spring and Autumn Annals.

"But there've been no sage emperors since then, only these august lords indulging themselves with such abandon.

Pundits go around talking nonsense, filling all beneath Heaven with the claims of Yang Chu and Mo Tzu: if there's a doctrine that can't be traced back to Yang, it can surely be traced back to Mo. Yang's school preaches *everyone for themselves,* and so denies the sovereign. Mo's school preaches *loving everyone equally,* and so denies the father. No father and no sovereign – that's the realm of birds and animals.

"Kung-ming Yi said: *There's plenty of juicy meat in your kitchen and plenty of well-fed horses in your stable – but the people here look hungry, and in the countryside they're starving to death. You're feeding humans to animals.* Unless the Way of Yang and Mo withers and the Way of Confucius flourishes, twisty words will keep deluding the people and blocking the path of Humanity and Duty. When Humanity and Duty are blocked up, humans are fed to animals. And pretty soon humans will be feeding on humans. I'm heartsick over it all, and so guard the Way of ancient sages. If we resist Yang and Mo, driving their reckless ideas away, those pundits will stop spreading their twisty words. Born of the mind, such things cripple our endeavors, and then our endeavors cripple government. If ever great sages arise again, they won't question what I've said.

"In ancient times, Yü controlled the floodwaters and brought peace to all beneath Heaven. Duke Chou subjugated the wild tribes of the east and north, drove the fierce animals away, and brought peace of mind to the people. When Confucius finished *The Spring and Autumn Annals,* rebellious ministers and thieving sons were filled with fear.

"The *Book of Songs* says:

> *fighting down the wild tribes*
> *and punishing Ch'u and Shu.*
> *And so no one dares resist us.*

No father and no sovereign – this is what Duke Chou fought against. And so, continuing the work of the three sages, I want to rectify people's minds and put an end to twisty words, resist dangerous conduct and drive reckless ideas away. It isn't that I love to argue. I just can't see how to avoid it, for only those who speak out against Yang and Mo are true followers of the sages."

10 K'uang Chang[9] said: "Isn't Master Chung a man of utterly pure principles? A recluse in the wilds of Wu Ling, he once had nothing to eat for three days, which robbed him of hearing and sight. There was a plum tree standing beside his well, dung worms eating at its fruit. He crawled over to it and began eating too. He took three bites, and suddenly he could hear and see again."

"Surely Master Chung is the finest man in the nation of

Ch'i," replied Mencius. "But still, how can he be called a man of pure principles? To master his discipline completely, you'd have to be an earthworm – eating leaf rot up above and drinking from the Yellow Springs of graveland down below.

"Was Chung's house built by the great recluse Po Yi or the great bandit Chih? And was his millet grown by Po Yi, or Chih the bandit? How could he know?"

"What difference does it make?" countered K'uang Chang. "He wove sandals with hemp spun by his wife, and they bartered them for the things they needed."

"Master Chung comes from an old and noble family of Ch'i," said Mencius. "His brother's lofty position earned him ten thousand measures of grain. But Chung thought his brother only earned that grain by ignoring Duty, so he refused to eat it. And he thought his brother only paid for his house by ignoring Duty, so he refused to stay in it. Instead, he lived in Wu Ling, far from his brother and mother.

"One day he returned home and found that his brother had been given a live goose by someone wanting favors. He frowned and said: *What good is this cackling creature to you?* A few days later, his mother killed the goose and served it to Chung for dinner. Having been away, his brother returned just then and said: *Isn't this the meat of that cackling goose?* Chung thereupon ran outside and threw it up.

"He never again ate his mother's food, but he ate his wife's. He never again lived in his brother's house, but he lived in his Wu Ling house. So did he perfect that way of life completely? Only an earthworm could master Chung's discipline completely."

VII

1 Mencius said: "Even with the sharp eyes of Li Lou and the skill of Master Kung-shu, you need a compass and square to render circles and squares true. Even with the penetrating ear of Maestro K'uang, you need the six pitch-pipes to tune the five notes true. And even with the Way of emperors Yao and Shun mastered, you need Humane government to govern all beneath Heaven in justice.

"There may be rulers today renowned for their Humanity, but they're neither blessings to the people nor beacons to future generations, for they aren't furthering the Way of ancient emperors. Hence it is said:

> *Virtue alone isn't enough for government,*
> *and law cannot alone put itself into action.*

And the *Songs* say:

> *Never transgress and never forget:*
> *always abide in the ancient rules.*

Has anyone ever erred by honoring the laws of ancient emperors?

"Having reached the limits of sight trying to render round and square, level and straight, the sage turns to compass and square. You can depend on them always. Having reached the limits of hearing trying to tune the five notes true, the sage turns to the six pitch-pipes. You can depend on them always. And having reached the limits of mind trying to let Humanity shelter all beneath Heaven, the sage turns to government that never oppresses the people. Hence it is said:

> *If you want to go high, begin atop hills and mounds.*
> *If you want to go deep, begin among rivers and marshes.*

So if you want to govern and don't begin with the Way of ancient emperors, how can you be called wise?

"That's why only the Humane are fit for high position: if the Inhumane hold high position, evil is sown among the people. When the Way isn't in a leader's thoughts, officials stop fostering the law. When the court doesn't trust the Way, workers don't trust principles. And when a ruler ignores Duty, the people ignore regulations. In such times, a nation survives on luck alone.

"Hence it is said:

> *If city walls are unfinished and weapons scarce, it doesn't spell disaster for the nation. If people aren't plowing new fields or piling up wealth, it doesn't spell ruin for the nation. But if a leader ignores Ritual and officials ignore learning, the people turn to banditry and rebellion, and the nation crumbles in less than a day.*

And the *Songs* say:

> *Heaven is dark with menace –*
> *stop this idle drift and chatter.*

Idle drift and chatter means *chitchat doing nothing.* To ignore Duty in serving the ruler, to ignore Ritual in taking office and renouncing office, to deny the Way of ancient emperors in your speech – that is chitchat doing nothing.

"Hence it is said:

> *To expect impossible achievements from a ruler – that is called honoring him. To open up his virtue and seal up his depravity – that is called revering him. But to excuse him as incapable of something – that is called plundering him."*

2 Mencius said: "The final perfection of circle and square is the compass and square. And the final perfection of human community is the sage. If you want to be a ruler, you must enact the Way of a ruler fully. If you want to be a minister, you must enact the Way of a minister fully. In either case, simply take Yao and Shun as your standard and you'll succeed. Unless a minister serves his sovereign the way Shun served Yao, he'll fail to revere his sovereign. And unless a ruler governs his people the way Yao governed his people, he'll do nothing more than plunder them.

"Confucius said:

> *There are two Ways: Humanity and Inhumanity. It's that simple. If a ruler tyrannizes his people ruthlessly, he will be killed and his nation destroyed. If he's less than ruthless in his tyranny, his life will be in danger and his nation pared away. Such rulers are given names like The Dark and The Cruel. And such curses are never changed, not even by a hundred generations of the most devoted sons and caring grandsons.*

"This is what the *Songs* are talking about when they say:

> *A warning to the Shang isn't far off:*
> *it's the last Hsia tyrant's overthrow."*

3 Mencius said: "When the Three Dynasties[1] practiced Humanity, they possessed all beneath Heaven. When they practiced Inhumanity, they lost all beneath Heaven. And when the nations of our time rise and fall, persist and perish – it's no different.

"When the Son of Heaven practices Inhumanity, he cannot preserve all within the four seas. When the august lords practice Inhumanity, they cannot preserve the gods of soil and grain. When high counselors and ministers practice Inhumanity, they cannot preserve the ancestral temples.

When officials and common people practice Inhumanity, they cannot preserve their own four limbs.

"To dread death and yet love Inhumanity – that is like dreading drunkenness and yet insisting on wine."

4 Mencius said: "If you try to love people but they keep distant, turn back to your Humanity. If you try to govern people but they resist, turn back to your wisdom. If you try to honor people but they don't reciprocate, turn back to your reverence.

"When you attempt something and fail, always turn back to yourself for the reason. Rectify yourself, and all beneath Heaven will return home to you. The *Songs* say:

> *Always worthy of Heaven's Mandate,*
> *he found great prosperity in himself.*"

5 Mencius said: "There is a saying the people keep repeating:

> *All beneath Heaven: nation: family.*

All beneath Heaven is rooted in nation. Nation is rooted in family. And family is rooted in self."

6 Mencius said: "To govern isn't difficult: Just don't offend the great families. Whoever the great families admire, the nation will admire. Whoever the nation admires, all beneath Heaven will admire. And so your Integrity and teaching will flood all within the four seas."

7 Mencius said: "When all beneath Heaven abides in the Way, small Integrity serves great Integrity, and small wisdom serves great wisdom. When all beneath Heaven ignores the Way, small serves large, and weak serves strong. Either way, Heaven issues it forth – and those who abide by Heaven endure, while those who defy Heaven perish.

"Duke Ching of Ch'i said: *We cannot give commands and we refuse to accept them – that is to be cut off from others and doomed.* And so in tears he gave his daughter to Wu as a bride.

"Now, even though small countries take large countries as their teachers in ruthlessness, they're too proud to submit to them. This is like disciples refusing to submit to their teachers. If you're proud, there's nothing like taking Emperor Wen as your teacher. Whoever takes Wen as his teacher will soon govern all beneath Heaven: if he begins with a large country, it will take only five years; and if he begins with a small country, it will take only seven.

"The *Songs* say:

The sons and grandsons of Shang
numbered over a hundred thousand.
But the Celestial Lord mandated it,
so they succumbed to Emperor Wen,
to Emperor Wen they succumbed.
Heaven's mandate is not forever:
Shang officials sure and bright
now pour libations in our temples.

And of this, Confucius said:

There's no outnumbering Humanity. If the ruler of a nation loves Humanity, no enemy in all beneath Heaven can stand against him.

Now, even though they want no enemy in all beneath Heaven to stand against them, rulers refuse to practice Humanity. This is like clutching hot metal without dousing it in water.

And who can clutch hot metal
without dousing it in water?

say the *Songs*."

8 Mencius said: "You can't talk sense to the Inhumane. They find repose in risk, profit in disaster, and joy in what will destroy them. If you could talk sense to them, would there be ruined countries and ravaged houses?

"A child once sang:

When the Ts'ang-lang flows clear
I rinse my hat strings clean.
When the Ts'ang-lang flows muddy
I rinse my feet clean.[2]

And of this, Confucius said:

Listen well, my little ones. When clear it rinses hat strings clean, and when muddy it rinses feet clean. The choice is its own.

And so, only after a person has demeaned himself will others demean him. Only after a great family has destroyed itself will others destroy it. And only after a country has torn itself down will others tear it down. The "T'ai Chia" says:

Ruin from Heaven
we can weather.
Ruin from ourselves
we never survive.

That says it exactly."

9 Mencius said: "The tyrants Chieh and Chou lost the people – that's why they lost all beneath Heaven. And it was in losing the people's hearts that they lost the people.

"The way to win over all beneath Heaven is to win over the people. The way to win over the people is to win over the people's hearts. And the way to win over the people's hearts is to surround them with what they want and keep them clear of what they hate.

"The people return to Humanity like water flowing downhill or animals heading into the wilds. Driving fish into them, otters serve deep waters; driving sparrows into them, kestrels serve thickets. And driving the people to them, the tyrants Chieh and Chou likewise served T'ang and Wu. If there were today a single ruler in all beneath Heaven who loved Humanity, the august lords would all serve him by driving the people to him. He may not want to be emperor, but how could he avoid it?

"Those who want to be emperor are like people who start searching for three-year-old moxa, hoping to cure a seven-year-old illness. If they haven't stored it away in advance, they'll have to suffer without it. It's like that with Humanity – if you haven't devoted yourself to it, you'll be hounded by worry and shame until you're finally caught in death's snare. The *Songs* say:

> *You'll never save this world,*
> *just sink into ruin together.*

That says it exactly."

10 Mencius said: "You can't talk sense to the reckless, and you can't help the suicidal. To refuse Ritual and Duty when you speak – that is called reckless. To believe you cannot dwell in Humanity or abide in Duty – that is called suicidal. Humanity is our tranquil home, and Duty our sure path. And how could anyone leave a tranquil home empty or a sure path untraveled?"

11 Mencius said: "The Way is close at hand but sought far off. Essentials are easy but sought in the difficult.

"If people all treated family as family and elders as elders, all beneath Heaven would be at peace."

12 Mencius said: "If a common official cannot inspire a sovereign's trust, he'll never win over the people and

govern them. But there's a Way to inspire a sovereign's trust. If you can't inspire trust in your friends, you'll never inspire trust in your sovereign. But there's a Way to inspire trust in your friends. If in serving your family you can't bring them joy, you'll never inspire trust in your friends. There's a Way to bring joy to your family. If you look within and find you aren't faithful to yourself, you'll never please your family. But there's a Way to be faithful to yourself. If you cannot render benevolence clear in the world, you'll never be faithful to yourself.

"Hence, the Way of Heaven is in faithful things, and the Way of humankind is in faithful thought. If you're faithful to yourself, you cannot fail to inspire others. And if you aren't faithful to yourself, you'll never inspire others."

13 Mencius said: "Po Yi fled the tyrant Chou and settled on the shores of the North Sea. On hearing that Emperor Wen had come to power, he said *I hear Wen takes good care of the old, so why not go back and serve him?* Duke T'ai[3] fled the tyrant Chou and settled on the shores of the West Sea. On hearing that Emperor Wen had come to power, he said *I hear Wen takes good care of the old, so why not go back and serve him?*

"These two were the grandest old men in all beneath

Heaven. When they returned to him, they were the fathers of all beneath Heaven returning. And when the fathers of all beneath Heaven return to him, where else would the children go? Now if one of our august lords governed the way Emperor Wen did, it wouldn't even be seven years before he governed all beneath Heaven."

14 Mencius said: "When Jan Ch'iu[4] was governor for the Chi family, he wasn't able to raise their Integrity the least bit. Meanwhile, he managed to double the tax people had to pay. So Confucius said: *He's no follower of mine. If you sounded the drums and attacked him, my little ones, it wouldn't be such a bad thing.*

"It's clear from this that Confucius deplored anyone enriching a ruler who didn't practice Humane government. And he deplored even more those who waged war for such a ruler. In wars for land, the dead crowd the countryside. In wars for cities, the dead fill the cities. This is called helping the land feed on human flesh. Death is not punishment enough for such acts.

"Hence, those who excel at war should receive the highest punishment. Next come those who form the august lords into alliances. And finally those who open up wild land hoping to increase profits."

15 Mencius said: "Nothing reflects the person so well as the eyes. The eyes won't hide the evil in a person. If a person's heart is noble, their eyes are bright and clear. If it is not, their eyes are dark and cloudy. To hear a person's words, look into their eyes – then they can hide nothing."

16 Mencius said: "The dignified never demean others. The thrifty never rob others. A ruler who demeans and robs others can only worry that the people might turn on him – so how can he be dignified or thrifty? Sweet words and smiling faces – how can that make them dignified or thrifty?"

17 Ch'un-yü K'un[5] said: "When men and women give and receive, is it a violation of Ritual for them to touch?"

"It is," replied Mencius.

"If your sister-in-law was drowning, would you reach out your hand to rescue her?"

"If a sister-in-law was drowning, it would be vicious not to rescue her. When men and women give and receive, it's a violation of Ritual for them to touch. But reaching out your hand to rescue a drowning sister-in-law – it's the only choice you have."

"All beneath Heaven is drowning," continued Ch'un-yü K'un. "Why don't you reach out and rescue it?"

"To rescue all beneath Heaven from drowning, you need the Way. To rescue a sister-in-law, you need only a hand. Do you think a hand is enough to rescue all beneath Heaven?"

18 Kung-sun Ch'ou said: "Why is it the noble-minded never teach their own children?"

"The way people are, it's impossible," replied Mencius. "A teacher's task is to perfect the student, and if the student doesn't improve, the teacher gets angry. When the teacher gets angry, the student in turn feels hurt: *You demand perfection, but you're nowhere near perfect yourself.* So father and son would only hurt each other. And it's a tragedy when fathers and sons hurt each other.

"The ancients taught each other's children. That way father and son never demand perfect virtue of one another. If they demand perfect virtue of one another, they grow distant. And nothing is more ominous than fathers and sons grown distant from one another."

19 Mencius said: "Isn't family the most important thing to serve? And isn't character the most important thing to preserve? I've heard of refusing to squander your character in order to serve your family. But I've never heard of squandering your character in order to serve your family.

"There's no end to what we should serve, but serving family is the basis of all service. And there's no end to what we should preserve, but preserving character is the basis of all preservation.

"When Master Tseng was caring for his father, he always served wine and meat. When he cleared the table, he always asked who the food should be given to. And when his father asked if there were leftovers, he always said there were. His father died, and eventually Master Tseng was cared for by his son, Tseng Yüan. Tseng Yüan also served wine and meat, but when he cleared the table he never asked who the food should be given to. And when his father asked if there were leftovers, he always said there were none so that he could serve the food again. This is called caring for mouth and body alone. But Master Tseng's way is called caring for the essence. In serving family, Master Tseng should be your model."

20 Mencius said: "Admonitions aren't enough for them, and accusations aren't enough for their government. It takes a great man indeed to rectify the depravity in a sovereign's heart.

"When the sovereign is Humane, everyone is Humane. When the sovereign is Dutiful, everyone is Dutiful. And when the sovereign is principled, everyone is principled. Give it a principled sovereign and the nation is secure."

21 Mencius said: "There is the praise of those who demand little, and the derision of those who demand everything."

22 Mencius said: "Talk is easy when you don't have to get the job done."

23 Mencius said: "The trouble with people is that they fancy themselves great teachers."

24 Adept Yüeh-cheng went with Governor Wang Huan to Ch'i, and there he went to visit Mencius.

"So you've come to see me too?" wondered Mencius.

"Why do you ask that, Master?" replied Yüeh-cheng.

"How long have you been here?"

"I arrived yesterday."

"So is it surprising that I ask such a question?"

"But I haven't even found a place to stay yet."

"Is that what you've been taught – that you only visit your elders after finding a place to stay?"

"Yes, it was wrong of me," admitted Yüeh-cheng.

25 Mencius said to Adept Yüeh-cheng: "You've come with Wang Huan just to savor a little food and wine. All your studies of the ancient Way, and for what? A little food and wine?"

26 Mencius said: "There are three ways you can fail to honor your parents, and the worst is to have no heir. Shun married without telling his parents because he was afraid that he might have no heir. For the noble-minded, this is no different than telling them."

27 Mencius said: "The substance of Humanity is nothing other than serving your family, and the substance of Duty nothing other than obeying your elders. The substance of wisdom is to understand these two things and cleave to them always. The substance of Ritual is to shape and embellish these two things. And the substance of music is to infuse these two things with joy. Once joy wells up, how can it be stopped? And if joy can't be stopped, hands and feet soon strike up a dance of their own."

28 Mencius said: "Imagine all beneath Heaven turning to you with great delight. Now imagine seeing that happen and knowing it means nothing more than a wisp of straw: only Shun was capable of that.

"He knew that if you don't realize your parents you aren't a person, and that if you don't lead your parents to share your wisdom you aren't a child. He fulfilled the Way of serving parents completely until Blind Purblind, his depraved father, finally rejoiced in virtue. Once his father rejoiced in virtue, all beneath Heaven was transformed. Once his father rejoiced in virtue, the model for fathers and sons was set for all beneath Heaven. Such is the greatness of honoring parents."

VIII

1 Mencius said: "Emperor Shun was a barbarian from the east: he was born in Chu Feng, moved to Fu Hsia, and finally died in Ming T'iao. Emperor Wen was a barbarian from the west: he was born in Ch'i Chou and died in Pi Ying. They lived more than a thousand miles and a thousand years apart – but putting their principles into practice throughout the Middle Kingdom, they were like the matching halves of a jade seal. The first was a sage, and the second was a sage: their thoughts were identical."

2 Even though he was prime minister in Cheng, Lord Ch'an[1] ferried people across the Chen and Wei himself.

"He was certainly kind," said Mencius, "but he didn't know how to govern. If he'd built footbridges every year in the tenth month and cart bridges every year in the eleventh month, the people could have avoided the ordeal of fording rivers. In governing, the noble-minded clear their way of people. How can they help people across rivers one by one? It's impossible to govern by making people happy one at a time: there aren't enough hours in the day."

3 Mencius said to Emperor Hsüan of Ch'i: "If a sovereign treats the people like his hands and feet, they'll treat him like their stomach and heart. If a sovereign treats the people like his dogs and horses, they'll treat him like a commoner. If a sovereign treats the people like weeds and dirt, they'll treat him like an enemy bandit."

"According to Ritual," said the emperor, "ministers wear mourning clothes when they leave the service of a sovereign. What must an emperor do so that his officials feel that way?"

"Act on their admonitions and listen to their words," replied Mencius, "so blessings rain down on the people. When a minister must travel, send people to escort him across the border and send emissaries ahead wherever he goes to prepare the way. Then give him three years to return before you seize his house and fields. These are called the three Ritual courtesies. If you follow them, your ministers will wear mourning clothes when they leave your service.

"These days a sovereign never acts on a minister's admonitions or listens to his words, and so blessings don't rain down on the people. If a minister must travel, the sovereign arrests him or makes things difficult for him wherever he goes. And the day the minister leaves, the sovereign takes back his house and fields. This is called being an enemy bandit. And why would anyone wear mourning clothes when leaving an enemy bandit?"

4 Mencius said: "When scholars are put to death for no reason, high ministers should resign their office and leave. When the people are slaughtered for no reason, scholars should resign their office and move away."

5 Mencius said: "When the sovereign is Humane, everyone is Humane. When the sovereign is Dutiful, everyone is Dutiful."

6 Mencius said: "Ritual empty of Ritual, Duty empty of Duty – great people never practice such things."

7 Mencius said: "Let the realized nurture the unrealized and the talented nurture the untalented, then people will rejoice in having worthy fathers and elders. If the realized abandon the unrealized and the talented abandon the untalented, there won't be the least difference between the worthy and the debased."

8 Mencius said: "Once there are things you refuse to do, you have things to do."

9 Mencius said: "When you speak of the virtues another lacks, think of the trials you may yet endure."

10 Mencius said: "Confucius was not a man of extremes."

11 Mencius said: "Great people's words need not be sincere, nor their actions fruitful. They need only abide in Duty."

12 Mencius said: "Great people never lose their child's heart."

13 Mencius said: "To nurture the living is not such a great thing. But to nurture them dead and gone – that is a great thing."

14 Mencius said: "To fathom great depths, the noble-minded realize themselves in the Way. Once they realize themselves in the Way, they dwell at ease in it. Once they dwell at ease in it, they trust themselves to it deeply. And once they trust themselves to it deeply, they find its origins all around them. This is why the noble-minded realize themselves in the Way."

15 Mencius said: "Make your learning abundant and speak of it with precision, then you will speak of essentials."

16 Mencius said: "If you use virtue to subdue others, you'll never subdue anyone. But if you use virtue to nurture others, you'll soon nurture all beneath Heaven. No one is emperor over all beneath Heaven unless it submits with subdued heart."

17 Mencius said: "Words that defy reality are ominous. And it's ominous reality that confronts those who would obscure the wise and worthy."

18 Master Hsü said: "Confucius often praised water, chanting *O water! O water!* Why was it water that he praised?"

"Springs well up into streams," replied Mencius, "and cascade steadily down night and day, filling every hollow before flowing on to the four seas. Those rooted in a source are like this. That's why Confucius praised water.

"Those not rooted in a source are like water gathering during the autumn rains: ditches and gutters are quickly flooded, but they're always dry again in no time. So it is that renown beyond what they deserve makes the noble-minded uneasy."

19 Mencius said: "The difference between people and animals is slight indeed. Most people blur that difference: it's the noble-minded that preserve it.

"Shun understood the commonplace and looked deeply into human community. He never put Humanity and Duty into action, for Humanity and Duty were always there in his actions."

20 Mencius said: "Yü hated fine wine but loved good advice. T'ang kept to the middle way and didn't need

rules when appointing worthy officials. Emperor Wen cared for the people as if they were invalids and gazed toward the Way as if he'd never seen it. Emperor Wu never slighted intimates and never forgot those far away.

"Duke Chou hoped to combine the methods of these dynastic founders in his rule. When he encountered some difficulty or contradiction, he turned to them and sat through the night deep in thought. If he was lucky enough to resolve the question, he would sit and await the dawn."

21 Mencius said: "When all trace of the sage emperors had vanished, the *Songs* were no longer gathered from the people.[2] After they stopped gathering the *Songs,* the *Spring and Autumn* was written.

"Such chronicles are all the same: for Chin the *Annals,* for Ch'u the *Wooden Tiger* and for Lu there is the *Spring and Autumn Annals.* It tells of such figures as Duke Huan of Ch'i and Duke Wen of Chin, and it's written in the historical style. Of it, Confucius said: *I've stolen all its lofty principles.*"

22 Mencius said: "The influence of someone noble-minded lasts five generations, and the influence of someone small-minded also lasts five generations. I was

never a disciple of Confucius: I'm schooled in the clarity he passed on to others."

23 Mencius said: "When you can choose to take or not take, taking offends humility. When you can choose to give or not give, giving offends generosity. When you can choose to die or not die, dying offends courage."

24 P'eng Meng studied archery under Yi. Once he had mastered Yi's Way, he thought Yi was the only archer in all beneath Heaven better than he. So he killed Yi.

"Yi was himself to blame for this," commented Mencius. "Kung-ming Yi said that Yi seemed blameless, but meant only that his blame was slight. How could he be completely blameless?

"Cheng once sent Master Cho Ju to invade Wei, and Wei sent Yü-kung Szu in pursuit. Master Cho Ju said: *I'm too sick: I can't pick up my bow. Today I'll die.* Then he asked his driver: *Who's coming in pursuit?*

"*Yü-kung Szu,* replied the driver.

"*Then today I'll live.*

"*But Yü-kung Szu is Wei's finest archer. Why do you say you'll live?* asked the driver.

"Yü-kung Szu studied archery under Yin-kung T'o, replied Master Cho Ju, *and Yin-kung T'o studied under me. Yin-kung T'o is a man of great dignity, and so only chooses friends of great dignity.*

"Yü-kung Szu arrived and said *Why isn't your bow at the ready, Master?*

"I'm too sick: I can't pick up my bow.

"I studied archery under Yin-kung T'o, and Yin-kung T'o studied under you. How could I turn your own Way against you, Master? Still, I am here on my sovereign's business and dare not forsake it.

"Drawing four arrows, he struck them against the wheel of his chariot, breaking off their tips, then shot them into the air. Whereupon he turned and left."

25 Mencius said: "If the beautiful Lady Hsi wore filthy clothes, people would have held their noses and hurried past her. So it is that a man deformed by his depravity can fast and bathe himself so pure he's fit to perform sacrifices to the Celestial Lord."

26 Mencius said: "It's simple: To say anything about the nature of things, you must attend to the facts,

facts in their original form. The trouble with knowledge is that it keeps chiseling things away. If intellectuals were like Yü draining floodwater into the sea, there'd be nothing wrong with knowing. Yü succeeded by letting water have its way, and if intellectuals just let things have their way, knowing would be great indeed.

"Heaven is high and the stars distant – but if you attend to the facts, you can calculate solstice for a thousand years without ever leaving your seat."

27 Lord Kung-hang's son had died. When Wang Huan arrived to offer his condolences, people hurried over to speak with him. And when he took his place as Counselor on the Right, others hurried over to speak with him. Seeing that Mencius made no attempt to speak with him, Wang Huan felt insulted and said: "Everyone here has had some words for me. Only Mencius has failed to do me that courtesy."

When Mencius heard about this, he said: "According to Ritual, you don't leave your position at court to speak with others, and you don't break ranks to bow to others. I was only observing Ritual. Isn't it strange Wang would consider that an insult?"

28 Mencius said: "What makes the noble-minded different is that they keep their hearts whole. And to do that, they depend on Humanity and Ritual. Those who practice Humanity love people, and those who observe Ritual honor people. If you love people that way, people will always love you faithfully. And if you honor people that way, people will always honor you faithfully.

"Now suppose someone is treating me poorly. If I'm noble-minded I'll turn to myself, thinking *I must be neglecting Humanity. I must be ignoring Ritual. Otherwise, how could such a thing happen?* If I turn to myself and find that I am acting Humane and observing Ritual, but the poor treatment continues, I turn to myself again, thinking *I must be lacking in devotion.* If I turn to myself and find that I am indeed devoted, but the poor treatment still continues, I say: *This person is savage, absolutely savage: no different from an animal! Why should I keep troubling myself over such a creature?*

"This is how the noble-minded worry their whole lives through, and so never know unexpected disaster. They may have worries, but only worries like this: *Shun was a person, and I too am a person. Shun was an exemplar for all beneath Heaven, worthy to guide future generations, but I'm still nothing more than a common villager.* And that's a worthwhile worry, for what can you do about such worries? It's simple: be like Shun.

"The noble-minded never know disaster. If it isn't Humane, they don't do it. If it isn't according to Ritual, they don't do it. Therefore, an unexpected disaster is no disaster for the noble-minded."

29 In times of sage rule, Yü and Hou Chi passed by their own gates three times without entering.[3] Confucius called them wise and worthy. In evil times, Yen Hui lived in a meager lane with nothing but some rice in a split-bamboo bowl and some water in a gourd cup. No one else could bear such misery. But it didn't even bother Hui. His joy never wavered. Confucius also called him wise and worthy.[4]

Mencius said: "Yü, Hou Chi, Yen Hui – they all practiced the same Way. If anyone in all beneath Heaven drowned, Yü felt as if he himself had drowned them. If anyone in all beneath Heaven starved, Hou Chi felt as if he himself had starved them. And so they worked with fierce devotion. If the three of them had traded places, they would each have done as the other did.

"These days, if someone in your house gets in a fight, it's fine to rush out and rescue them with your hair hanging loose and your cap untied. But if it's someone from your village that's fighting, then it's wrong. In fact, it's perfectly fine if you just bolt your door and ignore it."

30 Adept Kung-tu said: "People all through the country talk about how poor a son K'uang Chang was. But you not only befriend him, Master, you treat him with gracious respect. How can that be?"

"It's common now for people to say there are five ways to be unfilial," replied Mencius. "Neglecting the care of parents because you're lazy – that is the first. Neglecting the care of parents because you love wine and *go* – that is the second. Neglecting the care of parents because you love wealth and adore wife and children – that is the third. Disgracing parents because you can't resist beautiful sights and sounds – that is the fourth. Endangering parents because you love valor and conflict – that is the fifth. Does Chang do any of these things?

"Chang and his father had a falling out because they tried to reform each other. Between friends, reform is fine. But between fathers and sons, it's a great destroyer of love. Don't you think Chang longed for the affections of husband and wife, child and mother? Once his father was offended, he wouldn't let Chang come near him. That's why Chang sent his wife away, banished his children, and lived his whole life without their loving care. He was convinced that his offense would be even greater if he didn't do that. That's the kind of man K'uang Chang is."

31 Master Tseng was living in Wu Ch'eng when some bandits from Yüeh invaded. Someone cried out: "Bandits are coming! Run!"

"Don't let anyone stay in my house or harm the gardens," Tseng commanded his housekeeper. Then, when the bandits left, he sent word: "Get the house ready. I'll be back soon."

Once the bandits had left and Tseng returned, his disciples said: "The Master has been treated with such sincerity and honor here. But when the bandits came, he ran first for all the people to see, and then returned only after the bandits had left. Doesn't that seem wrong?"

"Understanding such things is beyond you," said Shen-yu Hsing. "I once had trouble with people stealing hay, but it didn't involve any of the master's seventy followers."

Master Szu was living in Wei when some bandits from Ch'i invaded. Someone cried out: "Bandits are coming! Run!"

"If I run," replied Master Szu, "who'll help our sovereign defend the country?"

Of these things, Mencius said: "Master Tseng and Master Szu – they both practiced the same Way. Master Tseng was a teacher and elder; Master Szu was a common citizen of no importance. If the two of them had traded places, they would each have done as the other did."

32 Lord Ch'u said: "The emperor sent spies to see if you're really different from other people."

"How would I be different from other people?" exclaimed Mencius. "Even Yao and Shun were just like everyone else."

33 There was a man in Ch'i who lived with his wife and mistress. When he went out, he always came home stuffed with wine and meat. One day his wife asked who his companions were, and he told her they were all men of wealth and renown. So she said to the mistress: "When he goes out, he always comes home stuffed with wine and meat. I ask who his companions are, and he says they're all men of wealth and renown. But we've never had such illustrious guests here in our house. I'm going to follow him and see where he goes."

She rose early the next morning and followed him everywhere he went. But no one in all the city even stopped to talk with him. Finally he went out to the graveyard east of the city, and there begged leftovers from someone performing sacrifices. He didn't get enough, so he went to beg from someone at another grave. That's how he stuffed himself full.

The wife returned home and told the mistress what she'd seen, then said: "A woman looks to her husband for direction and hope throughout life, and *this* is what ours is like." Together they railed against their husband and wept in the courtyard. Later, knowing nothing of this, the husband came swaggering in to impress his women.

In the eyes of the noble-minded, when a man chases after wealth and renown, profit and position, it is rare that his women aren't disgraced and driven to tears.

IX

WAN CHANG *Book One*

1 Wan Chang said: "When he was working the fields, Shun wept and cried out to the vast Heavens. Why did he weep and cry out?"

"He was full of resentment and longing," replied Mencius.

"If your parents love you, you rejoice and never forget them," said Wan Chang. "If your parents hate you, you suffer but never resent them. So what is it Shun resented so?"

Mencius said: *"Now I understand Shun working the fields. But weeping and crying out to his parents and the vast Heavens – that I don't understand.* When Ch'ang Hsi said this to Kung-ming Kao, Kung-ming Kao replied: *Understanding such things is beyond you.* So he certainly didn't believe a worthy child could be indifferent enough to think *I work hard plowing the fields. That's all parents can demand of a child. If they don't love me, how could it be my fault?*

"To help Shun in the fields, Yao sent his nine sons and two daughters, his hundred officials, cattle, sheep, provisions in plenty. Officials throughout all beneath Heaven turned to him. Yao was about to give all beneath Heaven over to his care. But not being in accord with his parents, Shun was like a man so poor he had no home to return to.

"Everyone wants to have officials throughout all beneath Heaven rejoice in them, but that wasn't enough to ease his worry. Everyone wants beautiful women, but even Yao's two daughters weren't enough to ease his worry. Everyone wants wealth, but even the wealth of all beneath Heaven wasn't enough to ease his worry. Everyone wants renown, but even the renown of being the Son of Heaven wasn't enough to ease his worry. People rejoicing in him, beautiful women, wealth, renown – all that wasn't enough to ease his worry. Being in accord with his parents – that was the one thing that could ease his worry.

"When we're young we long for our parents. When we begin thinking of beautiful women, we long for the young and beautiful. When we have a wife and family, we long for wife and family. When we're ready to serve, we long for a sovereign and burn with anxiety if we don't find one. Longing for your parents throughout life – that is the mark of a great child. To see a man who still longed for his parents at the age of fifty, I look to Shun."

2 Wan Chang said: "The *Songs* say:

How do you go about marrying a wife?
You first inform your parents.

No one should be a better example of this than Shun. How is it he married without first informing his parents?"

"If he'd told them, he wouldn't have married," replied Mencius. "A man and woman living together is a great bond of humankind. If he'd told his parents, he would have forsaken that great bond, and that would have been an act of hatred toward his parents. That's why he didn't tell them."

"Now I understand why Shun didn't tell his parents," said Wan Chang, "but how could Yao marry his two daughters to Shun without telling Shun's parents?"

"Yao also understood that if he told them there would be no marriage," replied Mencius.

"Shun's parents sent him to repair the granary," said Wan Chang, "then they pulled down the ladder and his depraved father set the granary on fire. They sent him to dredge the well, then followed him and sealed him in. His brother Hsiang said: *I'm the one who thought of a way to deal with my brother, the city-building sovereign. You can have his granaries, my parents, and his cattle and sheep. But his shield and spear are mine. His* ch'in[1] *and bow, are mine. And his two wives – they'll offer their comforts in my home now.*

"Later Hsiang went to Shun's house and found him there, sitting on his bed playing the *ch'in*. Blushing, he said: *I was worried and thinking of you, that's all.*

"And I am thinking of my people, replied Shun. *Help me govern them.*

"I wonder: didn't Shun realize that Hsiang was trying to kill him?"

"How could he not know?" responded Mencius. "But he was worried when Hsiang was worried, and pleased when Hsiang was pleased."

"So Shun was only pretending to be pleased?" asked Wan Chang.

"No," replied Mencius. "Someone gave a live fish to Lord Ch'an of Cheng. Lord Ch'an told his pond-keeper to put the fish in a pond and take care of it. The pond-keeper cooked the fish, then reported to Ch'an: *When I first let it go, it seemed confused by all that water. Before long it was savoring the vastness. And finally it disappeared into the distance.*

"It's in its element! It's in its element! exclaimed Ch'an.

"The pond-keeper left and said: *How can Lord Ch'an be called wise? I cooked his fish and ate it too, and he just says: 'It's in its element! It's in its element!'*

"So, to deceive the noble-minded, you must abide by their principles. It's impossible to trap them unless you use their own Way. Hsiang came in the same loving Way that Shun would have come, so Shun was truly pleased. Is that pretending?"

3 Wan Chang said: "Hsiang spent his days trying to kill Shun. So when Shun became the Son of Heaven, why did he only banish him?"

"He gave Hsiang a noble title and land," replied Mencius. "Some called it banishment."

"Shun sent Kung Kung to Yu Chou and banished Huan Tou to Ch'ung Mountain, executed San Miao at San Wei and imprisoned Kun at Yü Mountain," said Wan Chang, "and all beneath Heaven assented, knowing he was rooting out the Inhumane. Hsiang was brutally Inhumane, and yet Shun gave him a title and the lands of Yu Pi. What had the people of Yu Pi done to deserve that? How could a Humane man do such a thing: punishing innocent people so he could give his brother a noble title and land?"

"A Humane man never harbors anger or resentment toward a brother," replied Mencius. "He cherishes and loves him, that's all. Cherishing him, he wants him to enjoy renown; and loving him, he wants him to enjoy wealth. By giving Hsiang a title and the lands of Yu Pi, Shun let him enjoy wealth and renown. To be the Son of Heaven and let your brother live as a mere commoner – how could anyone call that cherishing and loving?"

"What did you mean when you said *Some called it banishment*?" asked Wan Chang.

"Hsiang had no power in his territory," said Mencius. "The Son of Heaven appointed others to govern and collect taxes there. That's why people called it banishment. Do you think Shun would allow him to abuse the people there? Shun still wanted to see him often, so he came to visit often. That's what is meant by:

> *He didn't wait for times of tribute:*
> *he welcomed him as the Lord of Yu Pi."*

4 Hsien-chiu Meng[2] said: "There is a saying:

> *Once rich in Integrity,*
> *you're subject to no sovereign*
> *and you're son to no father.*

Shun stood facing south at court. Yao, leading the august lords, faced north and paid him homage. Blind Purblind, Shun's depraved father, also faced north in homage. When Shun saw his father there, a troubled look came over his face. Confucius said: *At that moment, all beneath Heaven was in such danger, such utter peril!* I wonder about that – was it really true?"

"No," replied Mencius. "Those are not the words of a noble-minded man. They're the words of a villager from eastern Ch'i. When Yao grew old, Shun helped him govern. The *Record of Yao* says:

> *After twenty-eight years, Yao passed away. The people mourned three years as if they'd lost their mother and father. And no music was heard anywhere within the four seas.*

And Confucius said: *The Heavens have not two suns, and the people have not two emperors.* If Shun had become the Son of Heaven and led the august lords of all beneath Heaven in their three years of mourning, there would have been two Sons of Heaven."

"Now I understand that Yao was never Shun's subject," said Hsien-chiu Meng. "But the *Songs* say:

> *Throughout all beneath Heaven*
> *everything is the emperor's land,*
> *and to the borders of this land*
> *everyone is the emperor's subject.*

And yet, after Shun became the Son of Heaven, how is it Blind Purblind wasn't his subject?"

"That isn't what this song is about. It's about people who neglect their parents because they're devoted to the concerns of an emperor's government, people who say: *Everything here is the emperor's concern, and am I alone capable of it?*

"Therefore, in speaking of a song, never let eloquence obscure words, and never let words obscure intent. Instead, let your thoughts inhabit the intention, then you'll understand. In the *Songs*, "The Star River" says:

> *Of those who survived in Chou,*
> *there won't be half a person left.*[3]

If you just look at the words and trust what they say, there wasn't a single person left among all the people of Chou.

"For a worthy child, there's nothing greater than honoring parents; and for honoring parents, there's nothing greater than nurturing them with all beneath Heaven. To be the Son of Heaven's father – that is an honor indeed. And to nurture him with all beneath Heaven – that is nurturing indeed. That's what the *Songs* mean when they say:

> *Devoted always to his parents' care,*
> *great exemplar of the devoted child*

And *The Book of History* says:

> *He went to see Blind Purblind full of respect, veneration, and awe. And Blind Purblind finally understood.*

That is to be *son to no father.*"

5 Wan Chang said: "Is it true that Yao gave all beneath Heaven to Shun?"

"No," replied Mencius. "The Son of Heaven cannot give all beneath Heaven to another."

"Then who gave all beneath Heaven to Shun?"

"Heaven gave it to him."

"If Heaven gave it to him, did it also school him in the details of its mandate?"

"No. Heaven never speaks: it reveals itself only through actions and events."

"How does it reveal itself through actions and events?"

"The Son of Heaven can recommend someone to Heaven," replied Mencius, "but cannot compel Heaven to give all beneath Heaven over to that person. The august lords can recommend someone to the Son of Heaven, but cannot compel him to give that person a title. Ministers can recommend someone to an august lord, but cannot compel him to appoint that person a minister. In ancient times Yao recommended Shun to Heaven, and Heaven accepted him. Yao presented Shun to the people, and the people accepted him. That's why I say Heaven never speaks: it reveals itself only through actions and events."

"Yao recommended Shun to Heaven, and Heaven ac-

selor, but Yi Yin was so perfectly content that he said: *What would I do with T'ang's lavish gifts? Why should I stop dwelling in these fields, delighting in the Way of Yao and Shun?* Only after T'ang had sent three invitations did Yi Yin finally agree, saying: *I could go on dwelling in these fields, delighting in the Way of Yao and Shun, but wouldn't it be better to turn this sovereign into another Yao or Shun? Wouldn't it be better to turn our people into another nation of Yao or Shun, to see this happen with my own eyes? Having brought this people into being, Heaven appointed the wise to awaken those who will be wise, appointed the awakened to awaken those who will be awakened. Of Heaven's people, I am one of the awakened, so I should use this Way to awaken the people. If I don't awaken them, who will?*

"If there were any peasants in all beneath Heaven not enjoying the blessings of Yao and Shun, Yi Yin felt as if he himself had thrown them into a ditch. That's how deeply responsible he felt for all beneath Heaven. So he went to T'ang and counseled him to invade Hsia and rescue its people.

"I've never heard of straightening others by bending yourself, let alone straightening all beneath Heaven by disgracing yourself. Sages all have their own methods: some are recluses and some statesmen, some leave and some stay. But these methods all return to the same place: keeping yourself pure.

"I've heard that Yi Yin used the Way of Yao and Shun to

earn T'ang's admiration, not that he used his marvelous cooking. In "The Councils of Yi," Yi Yin says:

> *Heaven's vengeance sprang from depravity in the Hsia palace. Our role sprang from nobility in our Shang palace."*

8 Wan Chang asked: "Some people say Confucius stayed with Yung Chü in Wei and the eunuch Chi Huan in Ch'i. Is that true?"

"No," replied Mencius. "That isn't what happened. Some busybody cooked that up. In Wei, Confucius stayed with Yen Ch'ou-yu. In fact, Lord Mi's wife and Adept Lu's wife were sisters, and Lord Mi said to Adept Lu: *If Confucius will stay at my home, I'll make him a minister here in Wei.* When Lu told him about this, Confucius said: *The Mandate of Heaven abides.* Confucius took office according to Ritual and renounced office according to Duty. Through both success and failure, he always said: *The Mandate of Heaven abides.* If he'd stayed with Yung Chü or Chi Huan, he would have violated both Duty and the Mandate of Heaven.

"Confucius left Lu and Wei in disgust. Huan T'ui, the Minister of War in Sung, wanted to kill him, so he had to travel through Sung in disguise. Then, when he was in such

"Yao's son was depraved; so was Shun's. Meanwhile Shun was Yao's trusted assistant for many years, and Yü was Shun's, so their blessings had rained down on the people for a long time. Ch'i was wise and worthy, able to carry on Yü's Way and honor it. Meanwhile Yi was Yü's trusted assistant for only a few years, so his blessings hadn't rained down on the people for long. Yi was far from another Shun or Yü, and there was a great difference in how wise and worthy the emperor's sons were. Such circumstances are all acts of Heaven: people aren't capable of such things. When something's done, but no one does it, it's an act of Heaven. When something happens, but no one makes it happen, it's the Mandate of Heaven.

"For a common man to rule all beneath Heaven, he needs the Integrity of a Shun or Yü. But he also needs the Son of Heaven's recommendation. That's why Confucius never ruled all beneath Heaven. But if someone inherits all beneath Heaven, Heaven won't reject him unless he's a tyrant like Chieh or Chou. That's why Yi, Yi Yin and Duke Chou never ruled all beneath Heaven.

"Because Yi Yin was his trusted assistant, T'ang became emperor of all beneath Heaven. When T'ang died, T'ai Ting was no longer alive to succeed him. Wai Ping ruled for two years, and Chung Jen four. Then T'ai Chia[4] overthrew the laws of T'ang, so Yi Yin banished him to T'ung. After three years, T'ai Chia began to regret his crimes. He reproached himself and changed. There in T'ung, he brought himself into Duty and dwelled in Humanity. After another three years, having taken Yi Yin's admonitions to heart, he returned to Po.

"Duke Chou never ruled all beneath Heaven in the Chou Dynasty, and it was for the same reason that Yi never ruled in the Hsia and Yi Yin never ruled in the Shang. Confucius said: *With Yao and Shun, succession was through abdication to their chosen successors. With the founders of the Hsia, Shang and Chou dynasties, succession was hereditary. But for all, the principle was the same.*"

7 Wan Chang asked: "People say Yi Yin's cooking was marvelous and that he used it to impress T'ang. Is that true?"

"No," replied Mencius. "That isn't what happened. Yi Yin was farming in the countryside at Yu Hsin, delighting in the Way of Yao and Shun. He ignored anything that violated Duty or the Way, even if offered all beneath Heaven. He wouldn't even glance at it for a thousand teams of horses. If something violated Duty or the Way, he wouldn't offer or accept the merest trifle for it.

"T'ang sent lavish gifts, inviting Yi Yin to be his coun-

cepted him," repeated Wan Chang. "And Yao presented Shun to the people, and the people accepted him. But how did all this take place?"

"When he put Shun in charge of the sacrifices, the spirits welcomed them. This is how Heaven accepted him. When he put Shun in charge of the nation's affairs, they were well ordered and the people were at peace. This is how the people accepted him. So Heaven gave it to him, and the people gave it to him. This is what I mean when I say the Son of Heaven cannot give all beneath Heaven to another.

"Shun assisted Yao for twenty-eight years. People aren't capable of such things: only Heaven could have done it. And after Yao died and the three years of mourning had ended, Shun left for lands south of South River in deference to Yao's son. Even still, when the august lords of all beneath Heaven wanted an audience at court - they went to Shun, not Yao's son. When people had lawsuits to settle - they they went to Shun, not Yao's son. When choruses sang ballads of praise - they sang of Shun, not Yao's son. This is what I mean when I say it was Heaven. For only after all this happened did Shun return to the Middle Kingdom and take his place as the Son of Heaven. If he'd just moved into Yao's palace and driven Yao's son out, it would have been usurping the throne rather than receiving it from Heaven. That's why Emperor Wu says, in "The Great Declaration":

Heaven sees through the eyes of the people. Heaven hears through the ears of the people.

6 Wan Chang asked: "People say Integrity began crumbling when Yü allowed his son to succeed him rather than choose someone wise and worthy. Is that true?"

"No," replied Mencius. "That isn't how it works. If Heaven wants to give all beneath Heaven to someone wise and worthy, Heaven gives it to someone wise and worthy. If Heaven wants to give it to a son, Heaven gives it to a son.

"In ancient times, Shun recommended Yü to Heaven. He died seventeen years later, and when the three years of mourning ended, Yü left for Yang Ch'eng in deference to Shun's son. The people throughout all beneath Heaven followed him the way they followed Shun after Yao's death, rather than follow Yao's son. Yü recommended Yi to Heaven. He died seven years later, and when the three years of mourning ended, Yi left for the north slope of Ch'i Mountain in deference to Yü's son. But when people wanted an audience at court or they had a lawsuit to settle, they didn't go to Yi, they went to Yü's son Ch'i. And they said: *He's the son of our sovereign.* When choruses sang ballads of praise, they sang of Ch'i, not Yi. And they said: *He's the son of our sovereign.*

trouble, he stayed with the pure Mayor Chen and advised Chou, Lord of Ch'en.

"I have heard you can judge resident counselors by who stays in their homes, and you can judge visiting counselors by whose home they stay in. If Confucius had stayed with Yung Chü or Chi Huan, how could he be Confucius?"

9 Wan Chang asked: "Some people say Po-li Hsi bartered himself to a Ch'in herdsman for five sheep skins and tended this man's cattle – all to impress Duke Mu of Ch'in. Is it true?"

"No," replied Mencius. "That isn't what happened. Some busybody cooked that up. Po-li Hsi was a native of Yü. Chin offered jade from Ch'ui Chi and horses from Ch'ü, trying to buy safe passage through Yü so its armies could attack Kuo. Kung Ch'i advised against it, and Po-li Hsi said nothing. He knew that giving the Duke of Yü such advice was futile, so he left for Ch'in. He was already seventy when that happened. If he didn't know by then that it was vile to try impressing Duke Mu by tending cattle, how could he be called wise?

"But he knew advice was futile and so didn't offer any – wouldn't you call that wise? He knew the Duke of Yü was about to be destroyed and left before it happened – wouldn't you call that wise? He was appointed to high office in Ch'in, saw Duke Mu was capable of great things and so assisted him – wouldn't you call that wise? And as prime minister, he made Mu a beacon to all beneath Heaven, worthy of guiding future generations – who but a sage is capable of such things? To sell yourself in order to realize your sovereign – no self-respecting villager would do that. So how could a sage do such a thing?"

If there were peasants anywhere in all beneath Heaven not enjoying the blessings of Yao and Shun, Yi Yin felt as if he himself had thrown them into a ditch. That's how deeply responsible he felt for all beneath Heaven.

"Liu-hsia Hui wasn't shamed by defiled rulers, nor did he consider common positions below him. When in office, he always depended on the Way and never hid his wisdom. When dismissed, he bore no resentment. And suffering adversity, he remained untroubled. Living among villagers, he was so content he couldn't bear to leave. He used to say: *You are you, and I am I. Even if you stripped naked and stood beside me, how could you ever tarnish me?* That's why small minds grow broad when they hear the legend of Liu-hsia Hui, and the niggardly grow generous.

"When Confucius left Ch'i, he simply emptied his rice steamer and set out. But when he left Lu, he said: *There's no hurry, no hurry at all.* That's the Way to leave your parents' country. If it was wise to hurry away, he hurried away; and if it was wise to linger, he lingered. If it was wise to stay somewhere, he stayed; and if it was wise to take office, he took office. That was Confucius."

Then Mencius continued: "Po Yi was a sage of purity, Yi Yin a sage of deep responsibility, Liu-hsia Hui a sage of complaisance – but Confucius was a sage who understood for all things their proper time. You could say he gathered the great perfections into a single orchestra – everything from resounding bells to rustling chimes of jade. Resounding bells begin a performance, and rustling jade ends it. To begin a performance – that is the task of knowledge. And to end a performance – that is the task of a sage's wisdom. A good analogy for knowledge might be skill, and a good analogy for a sage's wisdom might be strength. When you're shooting from beyond a hundred paces and your arrow reaches the target, that is strength. But if it hits the mark, that is something else again."

2 Po-kung Ch'i asked: "How did the system of position and endowment work in the Chou Dynasty?"

"No one knows exactly how it worked," replied Mencius. "The august lords thought the system was hurting them, so they destroyed all the records. Still, I once heard a summary:

"The Son of Heaven held one rank, dukes another, lords another, marquises another, earls and barons together another: that's five grades in all. The sovereign held one rank, ministers another, counselors another, high officials another, middle officials another, low officials another: that's six grades in all. The Son of Heaven controlled a thousand square miles, dukes and lords controlled a hundred square miles, marquises seventy square miles, earls and barons fifty

WAN CHANG *Book Two*

1 Mencius said: "Po Yi wouldn't look at anything foul, and he wouldn't listen to anything foul. He never served a sovereign he disdained, and never governed a people he disdained. So he took office in times of wise rule, and he renounced office in times of chaos. He couldn't bear to live in a land where perverse government attracted perverse people, where living among villagers was like donning fine court robes to sit in mud and ash. So when the tyrant Chou came to power, Po Yi fled to the shores of the North Sea, where he awaited the return of purity to all beneath Heaven. That's why the greedy are cured of greed when they hear the legend of Po Yi, and the timid grow resolute.

"Yi Yin said:

> *Any sovereign I serve is that much more worthy, and any people I serve is that much more worthy. So I take office in times of wise rule, and I take office in times of chaos.*
> *And he also said: Having brought this people into being, Heaven appointed the wise to awaken those who will be wise, appointed the awakened to awaken those who will be awakened. Of Heaven's people, I am one of the awakened, so I should use this Way to awaken the people.*

X

square miles: that's four grades in all. Whoever controlled less than fifty square miles had no relations with the Son of Heaven. They were attached to the august lords and called *dependents.*

"The Son of Heaven's ministers were given the same amount of land as the august lords, his counselors the same as marquises, and his senior officials the same as earls and barons.

"There were a hundred square miles in a large nation, and its sovereign's endowment was ten times that of a minister. A minister's endowment was four times that of a counselor. A counselor's was double that of a high official, a high official's double that of a middle official, a middle official's double that of a low official, and a low official's equaled that of a commoner in government service, which was whatever he could have earned from farming.

"There were seventy square miles in a medium-sized nation, and its sovereign's endowment was ten times that of a minister. A minister's endowment was three times that of a counselor. A counselor's was double that of a high official, a high official's double that of a middle official, a middle official's double that of a low official, and a low official's equaled that of a commoner in government service, which was whatever he could have earned from farming.

"There were fifty square miles in a small nation, and its

sovereign's endowment was ten times that of a minister. A minister's endowment was double that of a counselor. A counselor's was double that of a high official, a high official's double that of a middle official, a middle official's double that of a low official, and a low official's equaled that of a commoner in government service, which was whatever he could have earned from farming.

"As for the earnings of farmers: Each man had a hundred acres of land, and with that land an outstanding farmer could feed nine people and a superior farmer could feed eight, an average farmer could feed seven people, a fair farmer could feed six, and a poor farmer could feed five. In government service, the earnings of commoners was likewise calculated according to their different abilities."

3 Wan Chang asked: "May I ask about friendship?"

"Don't try to intimidate with age or position or powerful relations," replied Mencius. "In making friends, befriend a person's Integrity. Friendship isn't about intimidation. Lord Meng Hsien led a house of a hundred war-chariots, and he had five friends: Yüeh-cheng Ch'iu, Mu Chung, and three others whom I forget. They were only his friends because they weren't of a noble house: if they had been, they wouldn't have been his friends.

tion and spout lofty words – that is a crime. And to represent the people in their sovereign's court without putting the Way into practice – that is a disgrace."

6 Wan Chang said: "Why would a scholar refuse to be under an august lord's protectorate?"

"It would be too presumptuous," replied Mencius. "According to the rites, an august lord lives within another august lord's protectorate only after he has lost his nation. So for a scholar to live within an august lord's protectorate would violate Ritual."

"But if a sovereign presents him with grain, should he accept it?"

"Yes."

"How can it be right to accept?"

"The sovereign always provides for his people."

"If he's providing for you, you accept. But if he's offering you a gift, you refuse. How can that be?"

"It would be too presumptuous."

"Why isn't the other presumptuous?"

"When gatekeepers and night watchmen do their jobs, they're earning a salary. When they don't do their jobs, they're accepting gifts. And that is irreverent."

"Say a sovereign sends provisions and they are accepted," said Wan Chang. "Why shouldn't such gifts continue?"

"Duke Mu asked after Master Szu often, and often presented him with sacrificial meat. But Master Szu was insulted. He hustled the duke's envoy out the gate, made two deep bows facing north, then refused the duke's gifts, saying: *I can see this sovereign wants to tend me the way he tends his dogs and horses.* Perhaps that's when envoys stopped coming with gifts. And how could anyone say that a ruler is pleased with someone wise and worthy if he doesn't appoint him to high office or even support him?"

"What must a nation's sovereign do if he wants to earn a reputation for supporting the noble-minded," asked Wan Chang.

"The sovereign should send something first with his greetings," replied Mencius, "and it should be accepted with two deep bows. But from then on, the granaries and kitchens should send grain and meat without any mention of the sovereign. Being expected to break his back bowing over and over for a little sacrificial meat – that's what bothered Master Szu. He didn't think that was how you supported the noble-minded Way.

"Remember Yao's treatment of Shun? Yao sent his nine sons to serve him, gave his two daughters in marriage to

should be no reason to make excuses. No, how can anyone accept a gift of plunder?"

"These days, the august lords extract wealth from the people just like thieving bandits," said Wan Chang. "Suppose they lend their gifts the virtue of Ritual occasion and the noble-minded accept: what would you say of that?"

"Do you imagine that these august lords would be punished if a true emperor appeared?" replied Mencius. "Do you imagine he would try to reform them, and then punish them when they don't change? To call anyone who takes something that isn't theirs a thief – that's pushing righteousness too far. When Confucius took office in Lu, people there fought over the kill after a sacrificial hunt, so Confucius did too. If there's nothing wrong with fighting over the kill, what could be wrong with accepting a gift?"

"He was like that?" said Wan Chang. "So he didn't take office to serve the Way?"

"He served the Way."

"If he served the Way, why did he fight over the kill?"

"Confucius tried to begin by rectifying the proper use of sacrificial vessels, and so put an end to loading them with such exotic foods."

"Why didn't he just leave?"

"He wanted to make a proposal that would indicate his

method. His proposal was entirely practical, so when it wasn't put into practice he left. That's why he never served any sovereign for even three years. Confucius served when he thought his proposals would be put into practice, when he was invited earnestly, or when a duke offered to support him. Confucius served Lord Chi Huan because he thought his proposals would be put into practice, served Duke Ling of Wei because he was invited earnestly, and served Duke Hsiao of Wei because the duke offered to support him."

5 Mencius said: "You don't take office just to escape poverty, though there are times that is reason enough. And you don't marry a wife just for the sustenance, though there are times that too is reason enough. When escaping poverty, decline high positions and wealth in favor of common positions and poverty. What positions are fitting for those who would decline high positions and wealth in favor of common positions and poverty? Gatekeeper or night watchman.

"When Confucius was the officer in charge of grain warehouses, he said: *I keep accurate records, that's all.* And when he was in charge of flocks and fields, he said: *I make sure the cattle and sheep grow strong, that's all.* To hold a common posi-

"This is true not only for someone who leads a house of a hundred war-chariots, but also for the sovereign of a small nation. Duke Hui of Pi said: *I've made Master Szu my teacher and Yen Pan my friend. But Wang Shun and Ch'ang Hsi – they attend me.* And it's true not only for the sovereign of a small nation, but also for the sovereign of a large nation. Think about Duke P'ing of Chin and the scholar Hai T'ang: Duke P'ing came to visit when Hai T'ang said *come,* sat when he said *sit,* and ate when he said *eat.* Even if it was only vegetables and broth, he ate until he was full. He didn't dare refuse. But nothing more ever came of it: Duke P'ing never shared the position Heaven gave him, never shared the responsibility Heaven gave him to govern, and never shared the endowment Heaven gave him. That's how a scholar should honor the wise and worthy, but not how a duke or emperor should honor the wise and worthy.

"When Shun went to see Emperor Yao, Yao offered him the reserve palace and entertained him lavishly. Sometimes he was Shun's host, and sometimes his guest. This is an instance of the Son of Heaven truly befriending a commoner.

"To revere a superior – that is called exalting the exalted. To revere an inferior – that is called honoring the wise and worthy. Exalting the exalted, honoring the wise and worthy – in principle they are one and the same."

4 Wan Chang asked: "In exchanging tokens of friendship, what is the proper frame of mind?"

"Reverence," replied Mencius.

"Why is it irreverent to refuse a gift?"

"If a superior presents you with a gift, it's irreverent to accept only after asking yourself *How did he come by this – was it honorable or dishonorable?* So you certainly shouldn't refuse such a gift."

"What if you refuse in thought rather than word – so even though you're thinking *To get this, he did such dishonorable things to the people,* you find some other excuse to decline the gift?"

"If he befriends you according to the Way and presents the gift according to Ritual, then even Confucius would accept the gift."

Wan Chang asked: "Suppose there was a bandit who robbed people outside the city gates. Would you accept his plunder as a gift just because he befriended you according to the Way and offered it to you according to Ritual?"

"No, of course not," replied Mencius. "In the 'Commission of K'ang,' Duke Chou says: *Everyone despises a person who murders and robs without any fear of death.* Such people are fit only for punishment: trying to reform them is pointless. This practice was handed down from the Hsia to the Shang, and from the Shang to the Chou. So by now, there

him. He sent his hundred officials, cattle, sheep, provisions in plenty – all to support him as he worked the fields. Then he appointed him to the most exalted position. That's what I'm thinking about when I speak of *how a duke or emperor should honor the wise and worthy.*"

7 Wan Chang said: "How can it be right to refuse a meeting with an august lord?"

"Scholars in the city are called *ministers of market and well,*" replied Mencius, "and scholars in the country are called *ministers of forest and field.* But both are deemed commoners, and according to Ritual a commoner doesn't presume to meet with an august lord until he has presented his token of credentials and been appointed to office."

"When a commoner is summoned to war, he goes to war. So when the sovereign wants to see a scholar and summons him to a meeting, how can he refuse to go?"

"Going to war is proper. Going to such a meeting is not. And why does the sovereign want to see him anyway?"

"Because he's so renowned, so wise and worthy."

"If it's because he's so renowned – the Son of Heaven wouldn't presume to summon his teacher, so how could an august lord? If it's because he's so wise and worthy – I've never heard of summoning someone wise and worthy whenever you want to see him.

"Duke Mu went to see Master Szu often. Once he asked: *In an ancient nation of a thousand war-chariots, how would the sovereign befriend a scholar?* Master Szu was insulted and said: *The ancients had a saying: 'Don't talk about making him your friend, just attend him.'* Being insulted, Szu was blunt: *In terms of position – you are the sovereign and I the subject, so how could I presume to be your friend? In terms of Integrity – you should be attending me, so how could you be my friend?* If that ruler of a thousand war-chariots couldn't even make a scholar his friend, how could he hope to summon such a man?

"Once when he was out hunting, Duke Ching of Ch'i summoned his gamekeeper with a plume-crested flag. The gamekeeper didn't come, so the duke wanted to have him executed, but Confucius said: *A man of great resolve never forgets that he could be abandoned to ditches and gutters, and a man of great valor never forgets that he could lose his head.* The gamekeeper wasn't entitled to such a lofty summons, so he didn't answer it – that's what Confucius admired."

"How should gamekeepers be summoned?" asked Wan Chang.

"With leather caps," replied Mencius. "Commoners should be summoned with plain banners on bent-top staffs,

1 Master Kao said: "The nature of things is like willow wood, and Duty is like cups and bowls. Shaping human nature into Humanity and Duty is like shaping willow wood into cups and bowls."

"Do you follow the nature of willow wood to shape cups and bowls," replied Mencius, "or do you maul it? If you maul willow wood to make cups and bowls, then I guess you maul human nature to make Humanity and Duty. It's talk like yours that will lead people to ravage Humanity and Duty throughout all beneath Heaven."

2 Master Kao said: "The nature of things is like swirling water: channel it east and it flows east, channel it west and it flows west. And human nature too is like water: it doesn't choose between good and evil any more than water chooses between east and west."

"It's true that water doesn't choose between east and west," replied Mencius, "but doesn't it choose between high and low? Human nature is inherently good, just like water

"Why so surprised? You asked, and I wouldn't dare be less than honest and forthright with you."

After he'd recovered his color, the emperor asked about ministers from common families, and Mencius said: "If the sovereign is making mistakes, they admonish him. If they have to admonish him over and over, and he still refuses to listen – they resign and leave his country behind."

XI

scholars with dragon banners, and high ministers with plume-crested flags. When the gamekeeper was summoned with the summons due a high minister, he preferred death to the presumption of answering. If a commoner is summoned with the summons due a scholar, how could he presume to answer? And that's nothing like a wise and worthy man being summoned with a summons due the unwise and unworthy.

"Wanting to see such a man while not abiding by the Way – that's like inviting someone in while closing the gate. Duty is the road, and Ritual the gate. Only the noble-minded can follow this road, going in and out the gate with ease. The *Songs* say:

> *Chou's Way is whetstone smooth,*
> *and it's straight as an arrow:*
> *the noble-minded travel upon it;*
> *the small-minded gaze upon it."*

"When summoned by the sovereign," said Wan Chang, "Confucius didn't wait for a carriage to set out. Does that mean Confucius did wrong?"

"Confucius had taken office and so had responsibilities," replied Mencius. "And he was called with the summons due his position."

8 Speaking to Wan Chang, Mencius said: "Noble scholars in one village befriend noble scholars in another village. Noble scholars in one country befriend noble scholars in another country. Noble scholars throughout all beneath Heaven befriend noble scholars throughout all beneath Heaven. And when the friendship of noble scholars throughout all beneath Heaven isn't enough, we can also rise to converse with the lofty ancients. How can we fail to know them utterly by chanting their poems and reading their words? And we also converse with their age that way. That is lofty friendship."

9 Emperor Hsüan of Ch'i asked about ministers, and Mencius said: "What kind of minister are you asking about?"

"Is there more than one kind?" asked the emperor.

"Yes," replied Mencius. "There are ministers from royal families and there are ministers from common families."

"May I ask about ministers from royal families?"

"If the sovereign is making grave mistakes, they admonish him. If they have to admonish him over and over, and he still refuses to listen – they replace him."

The emperor blanched at this, so Mencius continued:

flows inherently downhill. There's no such thing as a person who isn't good, just as there's no water that doesn't flow downhill.

"Think about water: if you slap it, you can make it jump over your head; and if you push and shove, you can make it stay on a mountain. But what does this have to do with the nature of water? It's only responding to the forces around it. It's like that for people too: you can make them evil, but that says nothing about human nature."

3 Master Kao said: "*The nature of things* means *that which is inborn.*"

"*The nature of things* means *that which is inborn,*" repeated Mencius. "Just like *white* means *that which is white?*"

"Yes."

"So is the whiteness of a white feather the same as the whiteness of white snow? And is the whiteness of white snow the same as the whiteness of white jade?"

"Yes."

"Then is the nature of a dog the same as the nature of an ox? And is the nature of an ox the same as the nature of a human?"

4 Master Kao said: "Hunger for food and sex – that is nature. Then there's Humanity, which is internal not external; and Duty, which is external not internal."

"Why do you say Humanity is internal and Duty is external?" asked Mencius.

"Suppose there was an elder and I treated him with the honor due an elder," replied Master Kao, "it isn't because the honor due elders is somehow within me. It's like seeing something white as white: the whiteness is outside us. That's why I call Duty external."

"The whiteness of a white horse is no different from the whiteness of a white-haired person," said Mencius. "But doesn't the elderliness of an elderly horse mean something quite different to us than the elderliness of an elderly person? And which are you equating with Duty – the elder or the one who treats him with the honor due an elder?"

"I love my own brother, but not the brother of someone in Ch'in," said Master Kao, "so the reason lies within me, which is why I call Humanity internal. But I treat elders as elders, whether they're from Ch'u or my own family: so the reason lies within elderliness, which is why I call Duty external."

"But my enjoyment of roast meat is the same," countered Mencius, "whether I cooked it or someone from Ch'in cooked it. And it's like this for many things. So does that mean the enjoyment of roast meat is external?"

5 Adept Meng Chi asked Adept Kung-tu: "Why do you say Duty is internal?"

"I call it internal," replied Kung-tu, "because it's our reverence put into action."

"If someone in your village is a year older than your eldest brother, which do you revere?"

"My brother."

"In pouring wine, which do you serve first?"

"The village elder."

"First you treat this one with reverence, then you treat that one with the honor due an elder. So Duty derives from the external, not the internal."

Adept Kung-tu had no answer to this. Later, when he told Mencius what had happened, Mencius said: "Ask him which he reveres most, an uncle or a younger brother, and he'll say *An uncle.* Ask him which he reveres most, an uncle or a younger brother who's posing as the ancestral dead at a sacrifice, and he'll say *A younger brother.* Then ask what happened to his reverence for the uncle, and he'll say *It's because of the younger brother's position.* Then you can say: *If reverence is a matter of position, lasting reverence belongs to my elder brother, while fleeting reverence belongs to the village elder.*"

When Adept Meng Chi heard this, he said: "I treat an uncle with reverence as reverence is due him, and I treat a younger brother with reverence as reverence is due him. So Duty derives from the external, not the internal."

"In winter we drink broth," commented Adept Kung-tu, "and in summer we drink water. Does that mean drinking and eating derive from the external?"

6 Adept Kung-tu said: "Master Kao says: *Human nature isn't good, and it isn't evil.* There are others who say: *Human nature can be made good, and it can be made evil. That's why the people loved goodness when Wen and Wu ruled, and they loved cruelty when Yu and Li ruled.* And there are still others who say: *Human nature is inborn: some people are good and some evil. That's why a Hsiang could have Yao as his ruler, a Shun could have Blind Purblind as his father, a Lord Ch'i of Wei and Prince Pi Kan could have the tyrant Chou as their nephew and sovereign.*

"But you say: *Human nature is good.* Does that mean all the others are wrong?"

"We are, by constitution, capable of being good," replied Mencius. "That's what I mean by good. If someone's evil, it can't be blamed on inborn capacities. We all have a heart of compassion and a heart of conscience, a heart of reverence and a heart of right and wrong. In a heart of compassion is Humanity, and in a heart of conscience is Duty. In a heart of reverence is Ritual, and in a heart of right and wrong is wisdom. Humanity, Duty, Ritual, wisdom – these are not external things we meld into us. They're part of us from the beginning, though we may not realize it. Hence the saying: *What you seek you will find, and what you ignore you will lose.* Some make more of themselves than others, maybe two or five or countless times more. But that's only because some people fail to realize their inborn capacities.

"The *Songs* say:

Heaven gave birth to humankind,
and whatever is has its own laws:
cleaving to what makes us human,
people delight in stately Integrity.

Of this, Confucius said: *Whoever wrote this song knew the Way well.* So whatever is must have its own laws, and whenever they cleave to what makes us human, the people must delight in stately Integrity."

7 Mencius said: "In good years, young men are mostly fine. In bad years, they're mostly cruel and violent. It isn't that Heaven endows them with such different capacities, only that their hearts are mired in such different situations. Think about barley: if you plant the seeds carefully at the same time and in same place, they'll all sprout and grow ripe by summer solstice. If they don't grow the same – it's because of inequities in richness of soil, amounts of rainfall, or the care given them by farmers. And so, all members belonging to a given species of thing are the same. Why should humans be the lone exception? The sage and I – surely we belong to the same species of thing.

"That's why Master Lung said: *Even if a cobbler makes a pair of sandals for feet he's never seen, he certainly won't make a pair of baskets.* Sandals are all alike because feet are the same throughout all beneath Heaven. And all tongues savor the same flavors. Yi Ya was just the first to discover what our tongues savor. If taste differed by nature from person to person, the way horses and dogs differ by species from me, then how is it people throughout all beneath Heaven savor the tastes Yi Ya savored? People throughout all beneath Heaven share Yi Ya's tastes, therefore people's tongues are alike throughout all beneath Heaven.

"It's true for the ear too: people throughout all beneath

Heaven share Maestro K'uang's sense of music, therefore people's ears are alike thoughout all beneath Heaven. And it's no less true for the eye: no one throughout all beneath Heaven could fail to see the beauty of Lord Tu. If you can't see his beauty, you simply haven't eyes.

"Hence it is said: *All tongues savor the same flavors, all ears hear the same music, and all eyes see the same beauty.* Why should the heart alone not be alike in us all? But what is it about our hearts that is alike? Isn't it what we call reason and Duty? The sage is just the first to discover what is common to our hearts. Hence, reason and Duty please our hearts just like meat pleases our tongues."

8 Mencius said: "The forests were once lovely on Ox Mountain. But as they were near a great city, axes cleared them little by little. Now there's nothing left of their beauty. They rest day and night, rain and dew falling in plenty, and there's no lack of fresh sprouts. But people graze oxen and sheep there, so the mountain's stripped bare. When people see how bare it is, they think that's all the potential it has. But does that mean this is the nature of Ox Mountain?

"Without the heart of Humanity and Duty alive in us, how can we be human? When we abandon this noble heart, it's like cutting those forests: a few axe blows each day, and pretty soon there's nothing left. Then you can rest day and night, take in the clarity of morning's healing *ch'i* – but the values that make you human keep thinning away. All day long, you're tangled in your life. If these tangles keep up day after day, even the clarity of night's healing *ch'i* isn't enough to preserve you. And if the clarity of night's healing *ch'i* isn't enough to preserve you, you aren't much different from an animal. When people see you're like an animal, they think that's all the potential you have. But does that mean this is the human constitution?

"With proper sustenance, anything will grow; and without proper sustenance, anything will fade away. Confucius said: *Embrace it and it endures. Forsake it and it dies. It comes and goes without warning, and no one knows its route.* He was speaking of the heart."

9 Mencius said: "Don't make the mistake of thinking the emperor lacks intelligence. Even the most vigorous plant in all beneath Heaven cannot grow if given sun for a day then left to freeze for ten. I very rarely see the emperor, and as soon as I leave, a crowd shows up to freeze him some more. So even if a new sprout appeared, what could I do?

"*Go* is surely a minor art, but if you don't give it your single-minded devotion you'll never master it. GoAutumnal is the finest player in all the land. But suppose he tries to teach the game to two people. One listens intently, studying with single-minded devotion. The other listens, but he's dreaming of swans in flight, the heft of bow and tethered arrow, the shot. Although he studies beside the first, he'll never be anywhere near as good. Is that because he's less intelligent? Not at all."

10 Mencius said: "I want fish, and I also want bear paws. If I can't have both, I'll give up fish and take bear paws. I want life, and I also want Duty. If I can't have both, I'll give up life and take Duty. I want life – but there's something I want more than life, so I won't do something wrong just to stay alive. I loathe death – but there's something I loathe more than death, so there are disasters I won't avoid.

"If you want nothing more than life, you'll do anything to stay alive. If you loathe nothing more than death, then you'll do anything to avoid disasters. But there are things people won't do to stay alive, and there are things people won't do to avoid disasters. So there must be something we want more than life, and something we loathe more than death. And it isn't something that only a sage's heart possesses: everyone has it. It's just that a sage never loses it.

"A basket of rice, a bowl of soup: to take them means life, to leave them means death. If they're offered with threats and abuse, a wayfarer won't accept them. If they're trampled on, even a beggar won't bother with them. But people accept ten thousand measures of grain as salary without even asking if they're violating Ritual or Duty. What could ten thousand measures of grain mean to me? A beautiful house? The esteem of wife and mistress? The gratitude of friends in need? If I refused to accept something even to save my life, am I now to accept it for a beautiful house, for the esteem of wife and mistress, for the gratitude of friends in need? Can't these people stop themselves? They're throwing away their original heart. There's no other way to describe it."

11 Mencius said: "Humanity is the heart, and Duty the road. To stop following the road and abandon it, to let the heart wander away and not know enough to search for it – what a sad sad thing. When chickens or dogs wander away, people know enough to search for them, but when their heart wanders away they don't. The Way of learning is nothing other than this: searching for the heart that's wandered away."

12 Mencius said: "Suppose your fourth finger were gnarled and crooked, though not lame or painful. If there was someone who could straighten it, you'd think nothing of traveling all the way from Ch'in to Ch'u. That's because your finger isn't as good as other people's fingers.

"When your finger isn't as good as other people's fingers, you know enough to resent it. But when your heart isn't as good, you don't know enough to resent it. That's what I call *not knowing what is what.*"

13 Mencius said: "Consider a young tree, an *wu-t'ung* or *tzu:* anyone who wants to keep it alive knows how to nurture it. Meanwhile they don't know how to nurture themselves. How can they love a tree more than themselves? This is thoughtlessness at its worst."

14 Mencius said: "People love all aspects of themselves equally. Loving them all equally, people nurture them all equally. When there isn't an inch of their flesh that they don't love, there isn't an inch they don't nurture. There's only one way to know if people are good or evil: look at the choices they make. We each contain precious and worthless, great and small. Never injure the great for the sake of

the small, or the precious for the sake of the worthless. Small people nurture what is small in them; great people nurture what is great in them.

"Consider a gardener who nurtures the scraggly sour-plum and date-bramble, but neglects the magnificent *wu-t'ung* and *chia* – that's a worthless gardener indeed. If you neglect shoulder and back to nurture a finger, and don't even realize what you're doing, you're nothing but a reckless wolf. And if you're obsessed with food and drink, you'll be scorned as worthless because you're nurturing the small and neglecting the great. Even if you neglect nothing else in your obsession with food and drink, you've let your mouth and belly become so much more than just another inch of flesh."

15 Adept Kung-tu asked: "If we're all equally human, how is it some are great and some small?"

"Great people abide by what is great in them;" replied Mencius, "small people abide by what is small in them."

"If we're all equally human, how is it some abide by what is great in them and some abide by what is small in them?"

"The senses cannot think, and so ear and eye are easily deceived by things. And things interact together, which only makes it worse. It is the heart which thinks, and so understands. Without thought there is no understanding. Heaven has given us these two things: heart and senses. If you insist from the beginning on what is great in you, what is small cannot steal it away. This is what makes a person great without fail."

16 Mencius said: "There is the nobility of Heaven on the one hand, and human nobility on the other. Humanity, Duty, loyalty, sincerity, tireless delight in the virtuous – such is the nobility of Heaven. Duke, counselor, minister – such is human nobility.

"The ancients cultivated the nobility of Heaven, and human nobility followed naturally. Today people cultivate the nobility of Heaven only out of desire for human nobility. And once they win human nobility, they abandon the nobility of Heaven. This is delusion at its worst, and such people come to nothing but ruin in the end. "

17 Mencius said: "The heart we all share longs to be exalted. But the exalted is already there in us, though we may not realize it. What people exalt is not the truly exalted. What some mighty lord exalts today, he may scorn as worthless tomorrow.

"The *Songs* say

> *we've drunk deep your wine*
> *and feasted on your Integrity,*

meaning that if you feast on Humanity and Duty, you don't long for the lavish flavors of sumptuous meat and millet. And if you're renowned far and wide, you don't long for robes of elegant embroidery."

18 Mencius said: "Humanity overcomes Inhumanity the way water overcomes fire. But when people wield Humanity these days, it's like they're throwing a cup of water on a cartload of burning firewood. When the fire keeps burning, they claim water can't overcome fire. This is the promotion of Inhumanity at its worst, and such people come to nothing but ruin in the end."

19 Mencius said: "The five grains are the finest of all plants. But if they don't ripen, they aren't even as good as wild rice-grass. For Humanity too – the essential thing is that it ripens well."

20 Mencius said: "Yi always shot from a full draw when teaching archery, and his students also shot from a full draw. A master carpenter always uses a compass and square when he teaches, and his students also use a compass and square."

XII

1 Someone from Jen asked Adept Wu-lu: "Which is most important, Ritual or food?"

"Ritual," replied Wu-lu.

"Which is most important, Ritual or sex?

"Ritual"

"What if using food for the Ritual sacrifice meant starving to death, and not using it meant having something to eat – would you insist on using it for the sacrifice? And what if observing the Ritual of claiming the bride in her home meant not marrying, and not observing it meant marrying – would you insist on claiming your bride?"

Adept Wu-lu had no answer. The next day he went to Chou and told Mencius what had happened. Mencius said: "It's easy. If you compare the tops without checking the bottoms, you can make an inch-long twig taller than a lofty tower. And if you say gold is heavier than feathers, you certainly aren't comparing a wisp of gold to a cartload of feathers. It's pointless to compare food and Ritual at a moment when food is vital and Ritual isn't: you can make lots of things seem more important that way, not just food. And it's pointless to compare sex and Ritual at a moment when sex is vital and Ritual isn't: you can make lots of things seem more important that way, not just sex.

"Go say this to him: *Suppose the only way you could get food was by twisting your brother's arm behind his back and stealing his food. Would you do it? And suppose the only way you could get a wife was by climbing over your east wall and dragging off the neighbor's daughter. Would you do that?*"

2 Lord Chiao of Ts'ao asked: "Is it true anyone can be a Yao or Shun?"

"Yes," replied Mencius.

"I've heard that Emperor Wen was ten feet tall," said Chiao, "and T'ang was nine feet tall. I'm nine feet four inches, but I have nothing but grain to eat. What shall I do?"

"Isn't it easy?" said Mencius. "Just act like Yao and Shun. If you can't lift a baby chicken, you are weak indeed. If you can lift three thousand pounds, you are strong indeed. And if you can lift as much as Wu Huo,[1] you're an Wu Huo. Why do people agonize over what they cannot do? They simply aren't trying.

"If you follow your elders, walking with dignity and respect, you can be called a younger brother. If you hurry ahead of your elders, you cannot be called a younger brother. How can anyone say they haven't the capacity to walk slowly behind? They just aren't trying. The Way of Yao and Shun is simple: act with the respect proper to a son and younger brother. If you dress the way Yao dressed, speak the way Yao spoke, and act the way Yao acted – then you're a Yao. And if you dress the way Shun dressed, speak the way Shun spoke, and act the way Shun acted – then you're a Shun. It's that simple."

"The Chou sovereign would listen to me and give me a place to live," said Chiao, "but I want to stay here, receiving your beautiful teachings with the other disciples."

"The Way is like a great highway," replied Mencius. "It's easy to find. People just don't bother to look. Go back to your home. Look for it there, and you'll find teachers aplenty."

3 Kung-sun Ch'ou said: "Master Kao claims 'Tiny Wingbeats' is the poem of a little person."

"Why did he say that?" asked Mencius.

"Because it's so full of resentment."

"Old Kao was awfully dogmatic about the *Songs,*" said Mencius. "Suppose a man from Yüeh drew his bow and shot someone: I might tell the story with a smile because the man's a stranger to me. But suppose my brother drew his bow and shot someone: then I'd be in tears when I told the story because he's my own flesh and blood. The resentment of 'Tiny Wingbeats' comes from the close bonds of family, for those bonds are themselves Humanity. Old Kao was impossibly dogmatic about the *Songs.*"

"Why is there no resentment in 'Gentle Wind'?

"In 'Gentle Wind' the parent's fault is slight, but in 'Tiny Wingbeats' the parent's fault is great. If you don't resent a parent's fault when it's serious, you're treating parents like strangers. And if you resent a parent's fault when it's slight, you're treating parents with abandon. Treating them like strangers, treating them with abandon – either is no way for a child to honor parents. Confucius said:

> *Shun was masterful in honoring his parents: at fifty, he was still longing for them."*

4 Sung K'eng was traveling to Ch'u. Meeting him at Chih Ch'iu, Mencius said: "Where are you going?"

"I've heard that war has broken out between Ch'u and Ch'in," replied Sung K'eng, "so I'm going to see the Ch'u emperor. I'll try to convince him to end the fighting. If I can't convince him, I'll go see the Ch'in emperor. I hope one of them will listen."

"I won't ask about the details, if you don't mind," said

Mencius, "but I would like to ask about the essence of your plan, and how you intend to convince these emperors to act on it."

"I'll show them how there's no profit in it."

"Your intent is noble, but your appeal misguided. If you talk to these emperors about profit, and in their love of profit they stop their armies - their armies will rejoice in peace and delight in profit. Soon ministers will embrace profit in serving their sovereign, sons will embrace profit in serving their fathers, younger brothers will embrace profit in serving their elder brothers - and all of them will have abandoned Humanity and Duty. When these relationships become a matter of profit, the nation is doomed to ruin.

"But if you talk to these emperors about Humanity and Duty, and in their love of Humanity and Duty they stop their armies - their armies will rejoice in peace and delight in Humanity and Duty. Soon ministers will embrace Humanity and Duty in serving their sovereign, sons will embrace Humanity and Duty in serving their fathers, younger brothers will embrace Humanity and Duty in serving their elder brothers - and all of them will have abandoned profit. When these relationships become a matter of Humanity and Duty, then the sovereign is sure to be a true emperor. So why mention profit?"

5 When Mencius was living in Chou, Chi Jen was the governor of Jen. As a token of friendship and respect, he sent Mencius a gift. Mencius accepted it, but without any show of gratitude. When Mencius was living in P'ing Lu, Lord Ch'u was the prime minister in Ch'i. As a token of friendship and respect, he too sent Mencius a gift. Mencius accepted it, but again without any show of gratitude.

Later, when he traveled from Chou to Jen, Mencius went to visit Lord Chi Jen. But when he traveled from P'ing Lu to Ch'i, he didn't visit Lord Ch'u. Adept Wu-lu was overjoyed at this, and said: "Now I see!"

"You visited Lord Chi Jen when you went to Jen," he said to Mencius, "but you didn't visit Lord Ch'u when you went to Ch'i. Is this because Lord Ch'u is a prime minister?"

"No," replied Mencius. "*The Book of History* says:

> *The gift is in the giving. If the giving isn't equal to the gift, it's like no gift at all, for the gift isn't invested with your good will.*

That is, it isn't a true gift at all."

Adept Wu-lu was delighted at this. When someone asked why, he said: "Lord Chi Jen couldn't leave his responsibilities and go to Chou, but Lord Ch'u could have gone to P'ing Lu."

6 Ch'un-yü K'un said: "If you consider fame and achievement primary, you serve the people. If you consider fame and achievement secondary, you serve yourself. You were one of the three high ministers, but you left before your fame and achievement had spread to sovereign and people. Is that really how the Humane act?"

"Po Yi lived in a humble position," said Mencius, "and refused to put his wisdom in the service of an unworthy ruler. Yi Yin approached both the noble T'ang and the tyrant Chieh five times. And Liu Hsia-hui didn't despise defiled rulers and didn't reject common positions. Each of these masters had his own Way, but they all shared the same goal."

"What was it?"

"Humanity. The noble-minded are Humane, so why must they share anything else?"

"Lord Kung-yi was prime minister in Duke Mu's time, Master Liu and Master Szu were counselors – but Lu lost territory faster than ever. Does this mean the wise and worthy can do nothing for a country?"

"When the nation of Yü ignored Po-li Hsi," replied Mencius, "it perished. When Duke Mu employed him well in Ch'in, the duke became the finest of august lords. Whenever countries ignore the wise and worthy, they don't just lose a little territory: they perish entirely."

"In ancient times," said Ch'un-yü K'un, "when Wang Pao settled at the Ch'i River, people west of the Yellow River became eloquent carolers. When Mien Chü settled in Kao T'ang, people in Ch'i's right-hand regions became eloquent singers. And the wives of Hua Chou and Ch'i Liang wept so eloquently for their husbands that they transformed the country's mourning traditions.

"What lies within reveals itself without. No one's ever been devoted to a purpose and had no achievements for the world to see. So there cannot be anyone wise and worthy among us: if there were, I would know of them."

"When Confucius was justice minister in Lu," said Mencius, "he was ignored. He took part in the sacrifices, but received no sacrificial meat, so he left Lu without even taking off his ceremonial cap. Those who didn't understand him thought he left because of the meat. But those who did understand him knew it was because Lu was violating Ritual. Confucius preferred to leave over a slight offense rather than wait for a grievous wrong. Commoners never understand the ways of the noble-minded."

7 Mencius said: "The five chiefs of the august lords were offenders against the three emperors. The august lords of today are offenders against the five chiefs. And the

high ministers of today are offenders against our august lords.

"When the Son of Heaven visited the august lords, it was called an Inspection Tour. And when the august lords went to the Son of Heaven's court, it was called a Duty Report. In spring, the purpose was to inspect the planting and provide whatever the farmers lacked. And in autumn, it was to inspect the harvest and help whoever didn't bring in enough. An august lord was rewarded with more territory if the Son of Heaven came to his domain and found the land opened up and the fields cultivated well, the old nurtured, the wise and worthy honored, and the distinguished serving in office. An august lord was reprimanded if the Son of Heaven came and found the land overgrown, the old abandoned, the wise and worthy neglected, and oppressors serving in office. The first time an august lord failed to appear at court, his rank was reduced. The second time, his territory was reduced. And if he failed to appear a third time, the Son of Heaven's armies removed him from power. Hence the Son of Heaven disciplined but never attacked. The august lords, on the other hand, attacked but never disciplined. Indeed, the five chiefs of the august lords often coerced august lords into attacking other august lords. That's why I say: *The five chiefs of the august lords were offenders against the three emperors.*

Duke Huan was the most illustrious of the five chiefs.

When he called the august lords together at K'uei Ch'iu, they bound a sacrificial animal and recorded their covenant, but they didn't trace their mouths with blood to consummate the covenant. Their first article stated: *Children who don't honor their parents shall be punished. Descendants shall not be set aside. Mistresses shall not be given the status of wives.* The second article stated: *Let Integrity shine forth by honoring the wise and nurturing the talented.* The third article stated: *Show reverence for elders, gentleness for children, and never forget the traveler and guest.* The fourth article stated: *Let no one hold office by hereditary privilege, and let no one hold more than one office at a time. In selecting officials, select only the most qualified. No ruler shall have sole authority to execute a high minister.* The fifth article stated: *Let no one build threatening earthworks. Let no one ban the sale of grain. And let no one confer land and title without the proper announcements.* The agreement also stated: *All who are united in this covenant shall hereafter live in harmony.* The august lords of today all violate these five precepts. That's why I say: *The august lords of today are offenders against the five chiefs.*

"Encouraging a sovereign's evil is nothing compared to the high crime of collusion in a sovereign's evil. The high ministers of today are all colluding in their sovereign's evil. That's why I say: *The high ministers of today are offenders against our august lords.*"

8 When the Lu sovereign wanted to make Lord Shen commander of his armies, Mencius said: "Sending the people to war without training – that is called ravaging the people. In the time of Yao and Shun, there was no toleration for a person who ravaged the people. It would be wrong even if Ch'i could be defeated and Nan-yang reclaimed, all in a single battle."

Lord Shen's face darkened, and he said: "I don't understand this at all."

"Let me explain it to you clearly," responded Mencius. "The Son of Heaven's territory covers a thousand square miles. If it's any less than a thousand square miles, he doesn't have enough to provide hospitality for the august lords. An august lord's territory covers a hundred square miles. If it's any less than a hundred square miles, he doesn't have enough to keep the canons of the ancestral temple.

"When Duke Chou was given Lu to rule, he had a hundred square miles. Still, it was plenty because he used it wisely. When Duke T'ai was given Ch'i to rule, he too had a hundred square miles. Again, it was plenty because he used it wisely. Today, Lu is five times a hundred square miles. If a true emperor arose, do you think Lu is one of those states he would pare down or one he would enlarge? A Humane person wouldn't even take what belongs to one state and give it to another, let alone kill people in his pursuit of land.

The noble-minded address fundamentals when they serve a sovereign: they make the Way his guide and Humanity his resolve."

9 Mencius said: "In serving their sovereign, people these days all say: *I'm expanding his territory and filling his treasury.* But what the world now calls a distinguished minister, the ancients called a plunderer of the people. To enrich a sovereign when he doesn't make the Way his purpose and Humanity his resolve – that is to enrich another tyrant Chieh.

"They say: *I'm forming alliances and winning wars for him.* But what the world now calls a distinguished minister, the ancients called a plunderer of the people. To strengthen a sovereign for war when he doesn't make the Way his purpose and Humanity his resolve – that is to empower another tyrant Chieh.

"When you abide by the Way of our times, leaving the practices of this world unchanged, then even if you're given all beneath Heaven, you won't keep it for a single morning."

10 Po Kuei said: "I'd like to see people taxed one part in twenty. What would you think of that?"

"Your Way is the Way of northern barbarians," replied Mencius. "In a nation of ten thousand families, would a single potter be sufficient?"

"No, there wouldn't be enough pottery."

"Northern barbarians don't grow the five grains, only millet. They have no city walls or buildings, no ancestral temples, no sacrificial rituals. They have no august lords, no diplomatic hospitality or gifts. And they don't have the hundred government offices and officials. That's why one part in twenty is enough tax for them. But here in the Middle Kingdom, how can we do without noble-minded leaders and the bonds of human community? If a country is crippled without potters, what happens without noble-minded leaders? If our rulers levy tax rates below that prescribed by the Way of Yao and Shun, they'll be nothing but barbarians great and small. And if our rulers levy tax rates above that prescribed by the Way of Yao and Shun, they'll be nothing but tyrant Chiehs great and small."

11 Po Kuei said: "I can manage high waters better even than Yü."[2]

"You're wrong," replied Mencius. "Yü's management of water is the very Way of water. And so he used the four seas as valleys to drain the floodwaters away. But you use neighboring countries. When you force water out of its natural course, it becomes a flood. And a flood is nothing less than a deluge, which is something the Humane despise. No, you're quite wrong."

12 Mencius said: "If the noble-minded are not faithful and sincere, how can they take command of a situation?"

13 The Lu sovereign wanted Adept Yüeh-cheng to preside over his government.

"When I heard this," said Mencius, "I was so happy I couldn't sleep."

"Is Yüeh-cheng a man of great strength?" asked Kung-sun Ch'ou.

"No."

"Is he a man of wisdom and foresight?"

"No."

"Is he a man of broad learning?"

"No."

"Then why were you so happy you couldn't sleep?"

"Because he's one of those men who loves virtue and benevolence."

"Is loving virtue and benevolence sufficient?"

"Loving virtue and benevolence is enough to govern all beneath Heaven," replied Mencius, "and what is Lu compared to that? If you love virtue and benevolence, people everywhere within the four seas will think nothing of a thousand miles: they'll come share their thoughts about virtue and benevolence. If you don't love virtue and benevolence, people will think your smug and arrogant manner says *I understand all things.* The tone and bearing of such smug arrogance – that alone will keep people a thousand miles away. And when worthy scholars stay a thousand miles away, people with flattering smiles and pleasing tongues come crowding around. Once that happens, how could anyone govern a country well?"

14 Adept Ch'en said: "In ancient times, when would a noble-minded man take office?"

"There were three situations where a noble-minded man would take office," replied Mencius, "and three where he would renounce office. First – he would take office when invited with reverence, according to Ritual, and told that his counsels would be put into practice. Then he would renounce office if his counsels were not put into practice, even if the Ritual courtesies hadn't been violated. Second –

he would take office when invited with reverence, according to Ritual, even if his counsels weren't put into practice. Then he would renounce office if the Ritual courtesies were neglected. Third – if he had no food morning or night, and so lived in such hunger that he couldn't walk out his gate, he would accept office if the sovereign heard about his plight and offered assistance, saying: *I've failed in the great work of putting his Way into practice, and I've failed to follow his counsels. Now if I let him starve to death in my domain, how could I live with the shame?* But in such a case, he accepts only to escape starvation."

15 Mencius said: "Shun issued forth from farmlands. Fu Yüeh rose from builders, Chiao Ko from salt and fish, Kuan Chung from jails, Sun Shu-ao from the sea, and Po-li Hsi from markets. So it is that whenever Heaven invests a person with great responsibilities, it first tries his resolve, exhausts his muscles and bones, starves his body, leaves him destitute, and confounds his every endeavor. In this way his patience and endurance are developed, and his weaknesses are overcome.

"We change and grow only when we make mistakes. We realize what to do only when we work through worry and confusion. And we gain people's trust and understanding only when our inner thoughts are revealed clearly in our faces and words. When it has no lawful families or wise officials within and no enemy threats without, a nation will surely come to ruin. Then its people will understand that through calamity and grief we flourish, and through peace and joy we perish."

16 Mencius said: "There are many ways to teach. I don't bother with teaching and instructing, but that's just another way of teaching and instructing."

XIII

1 Mencius said: "To fathom the mind is to understand your nature. And when you understand your nature, you understand Heaven. Foster your mind, nurture your nature – then you are serving Heaven.

"Don't worry about dying young or living long. What will come will come. Cultivate yourself well – and patient in that perfection, let it come. Then you will stand firm in your fate."

2 Mencius said: "Whatever happens is destiny, but we should accept only what is truly fated. Hence, one who understands destiny won't stand beneath a wall teetering on the verge of collapse.

"To fathom the Way in life, and then die – that is our true fate. To live tangled in fetters, and then die – that is no one's true fate."

3 Mencius said: *"What you seek you will find, and what you ignore you will lose.* Where this saying is right, and to

seek means to find, we're seeking something within ourselves.

"To seek is a question of the Way, and to find is a question of destiny. Where this is right, and to seek doesn't necessarily mean to find, we're seeking something outside ourselves."

4 Mencius said: "The ten thousand things are all there in me. And there's no joy greater than looking within and finding myself faithful to them. Treat others as you would be treated. Devote yourself to that, for there's no more direct approach to Humanity."

5 Mencius said: "To enact it without making it clear, to enact it over and over without inquiring into it, to enact it for a lifetime without ever understanding its Way – that's how it is for nearly everyone."

6 Mencius said: "It's impossible to be shameless. The shame of being shameless – that is shameless indeed."

7 Mencius said: "Shame is a great thing for people. Crafty schemers have no use for shame. And if you aren't ashamed of being inhuman, what will ever make you human?"

8 Mencius said: "In their love of virtue and benevolence, sage emperors of ancient times forgot about their exalted position. How could sage scholars of ancient times be any different? Delighting in the Way, they too forgot about exalted positions. So unless emperors and dukes came in reverence and according to Ritual, they were rarely admitted to see such scholars. And if it was nearly impossible to see them, how could those rulers ever convince them to take office?"

9 Mencius said to Sung Kou-chien: "You love to travel, offering your counsel to leaders, so I'll tell you something about such things: Know contentment when your counsel is valued, and contentment when it's ignored."

"What must a person be to know such contentment?" asked Sung Kou-chien.

"If you honor Integrity and delight in Duty you can know

such contentment," replied Mencius. "The worthy never forget Duty when destitute, and never abandon the Way when they succeed. Not forgetting Duty when destitute, the worthy realize themselves. And when they succeed without abandoning the Way, the people's faith in them never falters.

"When the ancients fulfilled their ambitions, bounty rained down on the people. When they failed, they were still worthy exemplars for all the world to see. Cultivate virtue and benevolence in yourself when destitute and alone. And when you succeed, share that virtue and benevolence with all beneath Heaven."

10 Mencius said: "A commoner only feels called to great work when an Emperor Wen appears. But a great man sets to work even when there's no sign of an Emperor Wen."

11 Mencius said: "To live humble and dissatisfied with yourself, even if all the wealth of Han and Wei were added to your own – that is the mark of a person beyond compare."

12 Mencius said: "If your Way is making life easier for them, the people won't resent hard work. And if your Way is helping them live, the people won't resent being led to their death."

13 Mencius said: "Under the finest of august lords, the people seem peaceful and happy. Under a true emperor, they seem utterly content. They neither resent him when put to death, nor praise him when richly rewarded. They grow more virtuous and benevolent every day, without ever realizing who makes this happen.

"So it is that when the noble-minded pass through a place, they leave transformations behind. And when they dwell in a place, they work miracles. They grace the same stream as Heaven above and earth below: who can doubt their healing power?"

14 Mencius said: "It's Humane music that goes deep inside people, not Humane words. And it's virtuous teaching that wins people over, not virtuous government. The people fear virtuous government, but they love virtuous teaching. Virtuous government can win people's wealth, but virtuous teaching can win their hearts."

15 Mencius said: "To have an ability without being taught – that is true ability. To know without struggling to know – that is true knowing.

"Young children all know love for their parents. And when they grow up, they all know respect for their elders. Loving parents is Humanity, and respecting elders is Duty. That's the secret. Just extend it throughout all beneath Heaven."

16 Mencius said: "When Shun dwelled deep in the mountains, he dwelled among trees and stones, roamed with boar and deer. The difference between him and the other mountain people was slight indeed. But then he heard a single word of virtue, saw a single act of virtue, and it was like a great river breaking through its banks: nothing could stop it."

17 Mencius said: "Don't do what should not be done, and don't desire what should not be desired. Abide by this one precept, and everything else will follow."

18 Mencius said: "Integrity, wisdom, skill, intelligence – such things are forged in adversity. Like the son of a common mistress, a forsaken minister is ever cautious, ever watchful. That's how he avoids danger and succeeds."

19 Mencius said: "There are people who find satisfaction in serving a sovereign. There are ministers who find satisfaction in keeping the gods of grain content. There are the denizens of Heaven who learn what will benefit all beneath Heaven and put it into practice. And then there are the truly great: they can rectify all things by rectifying themselves."

20 Mencius said: "The noble-minded have three great joys, and ruling all beneath Heaven is not one of them. To have parents alive and brothers well – that is the first joy. To face Heaven above and people below without any shame – that is the second joy. To attract the finest students in all beneath Heaven, and to teach and nurture them – that is the third joy. The noble-minded have three great joys, and ruling all beneath Heaven is not one of them."

21 Mencius said: "The noble-minded may want a large country and vast population, but that isn't what fills them with joy. To stand at the center of all beneath Heaven and bring contentment to people everywhere within the four seas – that's what fills the noble-minded with joy. But it isn't what answers to their nature. Their nature gains nothing if they manage the great affairs of state, and it loses nothing if they live in destitute obscurity. This is because the noble-minded know their given nature to be complete in itself.

"Humanity, Duty, Ritual, wisdom – such aspects of their nature take root in mind, flourish in appearance. There's a calmness in the face of the noble-minded, a calmness that also graces their back, radiates through their four limbs. And so the body of someone noble-minded speaks a parable without words."

22 Mencius said: "Po Yi fled the tyrant Chou and settled on the shores of the North Sea. On hearing Emperor Wen had come to power, he said *I hear Wen takes good care of the old, so why not go back and serve him?* Duke T'ai fled the tyrant Chou and settled on the shores of the West Sea. On hearing Emperor Wen had come to power, he said *I hear Wen takes good care of the old, so why not go back and serve him?*

When there's a ruler somewhere in all beneath Heaven who takes good care of the old, the Humane flock to serve him.

"When every five-acre farm has mulberry trees along the walls and a woman to raise silkworms, the old can wear silk. And when there are five hens and two sows, and their proper seasons aren't neglected, the old need not go without meat. When every hundred-acre farm has a man to till the fields, even large families don't go hungry.

"This is what they meant by *Wen takes good care of the old.* He organized farmlands and villages, taught people to plant mulberries and raise livestock, showed the women how to care for the aged. Without silk at fifty, people can't keep warm. And without meat at seventy, they can't get full. Not warm and not full – that is called freezing and starving. Among Emperor Wen's people, the old never froze or starved. That's what Po Yi and Duke T'ai were saying."

23 Mencius said: "If you expand their fields and reduce their taxes, you'll make the people rich. And if they use food according to season and wares according to Ritual, they'll never exhaust their wealth.

"People can't live without fire and water. But if you go knocking on gates at nightfall, asking for fire and water, no one will refuse you. That's because fire and water are so plentiful. In ruling all beneath Heaven, the sage makes beans and millet as plentiful as fire and water. When beans and millet are as plentiful as fire and water, how can any of the people be Inhumane?"

24 Mencius said: "When Confucius climbed Tung Mountain, he realized how tiny Lu is. And when he climbed T'ai Mountain, he realized how tiny all beneath Heaven is. So it is that once you've seen oceans, water seems petty. And once you've entered the gate of a sage, words seem petty.

"But there's an art to seeing water: look at its ripples, for the brilliance of sun and moon ignite anything that will hold light. And when water flows, it fills every hollow before moving on. It's like this for the noble-minded in the Way: they succeed only if the pattern they make is beautiful."

25 Mencius said: "To rise at the cock's cry and practice virtue and benevolence with untiring diligence – that is to be a follower of Shun. To rise at the cock's cry and chase profits with untiring diligence – that is to be a follower of Chih the bandit. There's nothing more to the difference between Shun and Chih than this: the distinction between virtue and profit."

26 Mencius said: "Yang Chu valued self above all: even if it would bring great profit to all beneath Heaven, he wouldn't pluck a single hair from his head. Mo Tzu proposed universal love: if it would bring any profit to all beneath Heaven, he would toil long and hard, wearing every hair from his body.

"Now we have Master Mo who clings to the middle ground. The middle ground is closer to the mark, but unless he allows for the complexity of circumstance he's still clinging to a single doctrine. The problem with clinging to a single doctrine is that it plunders the Way: to glorify the one, you cast out a hundred."

27 Mencius said: "The hungry savor any food. The thirsty savor any drink. They have no discrimination in food and drink: hunger and thirst has ruined it. And hunger and thirst can ruin more than people's tongues: it can also ruin their minds. Once you free your mind from the ruin of hunger and thirst, you no longer worry about failing to equal the great sages."

28 Mencius said: "All the wealth of three dukes couldn't make Liu-hsia Hui waver in his resolve."

29 Mencius said: "Getting something done is like digging a well. You can dig a well seventy feet deep, but if you don't hit water it's just an abandoned well."

30 Mencius said: "Yao and Shun possessed it by nature. T'ang and Wu embodied it. And the five chiefs of the august lords borrowed it. But if you borrow something long enough, who would know it isn't yours?"

31 Kung-sun Ch'ou said: "Yi Yin banished T'ai Chia to T'ung,[1] saying: *I can't be so intimately involved with someone who is so contrary.* The people were greatly pleased. And when T'ai Chia returned to Yi Yin a sage, the people were again greatly pleased. When a sage serves as minister under a sovereign who is not a sage, can he banish the sovereign?"

"He can if his motives are like Yi Yin's," replied Mencius. "But if his motives aren't like Yi Yin's, it's usurping the throne."

32 Kung-sun Ch'ou said: "The *Songs* say the noble-minded *never eat the food of idleness.* What do you think of

the noble-minded living on food they haven't grown themselves?"

"When a noble-minded man lives in a country and the sovereign values him," replied Mencius, "the sovereign gains peace and wealth, honor and glory. When disciples follow him, they learn to honor parents and elders, to earn trust and stand by their words. If there's anyone who *never eats the food of idleness,* surely it's him."

33 Prince T'ien asked: "What is the task of a worthy official?"

"To cultivate the highest of purposes," replied Mencius.

"What do you mean by *the highest of purposes*?"

"It's simple: Humanity and Duty. You defy Humanity if you cause the death of a single innocent person, and you defy Duty if you take what is not yours. What is our dwelling-place if not Humanity? And what is our road if not Duty? To dwell in Humanity and follow Duty – that is the perfection of a great person's task."

34 Mencius said: "If he were offered the state of Ch'i in violation of Duty, everyone believes Master Chung

would refuse. But this is only the Duty that refuses a basket of rice and a bowl of soup.

"There's nothing great about abandoning your place in the bonds of parent and family, sovereign and minister, leader and citizen. How is it people see something so small and believe it to be great?"

35 T'ao Ying asked: "When Shun was the Son of Heaven and Kao Yao was the justice minister, what would have happened if Blind Purblind killed someone?"

"Kao Yao would have arrested him," replied Mencius.

"But wouldn't Shun have forbidden it?"

"How could he forbid it? Kao Yao had been given authority."

"Then what would Shun have done?"

"Casting all beneath Heaven aside meant no more to Shun than casting aside an old sandal," said Mencius. "He would have stolen away with his father on his back, and gone to live beside the sea. He would have lived out his life happily there, forgetting all beneath Heaven entirely."

36 When Mencius was traveling from Fan to Ch'i, he saw the Ch'i prince and said with a sigh: "A dwelling-place transforms the *ch'i,* just as food transforms the body. Great indeed is the influence of a dwelling-place – for aren't we all alike born of humankind?"

Then he continued: "This prince's house, carriage, and clothes aren't much different from other people's. And yet he's so different. If his dwelling-place can do that, imagine dwelling in the most boundless dwelling-place of all beneath Heaven.

"The sovereign of Lu once went to Sung and called out at Tieh-tse Gate. Hearing him, the gatekeeper said: *This isn't my sovereign. How is it he sounds so much like my sovereign?* The reason is simple: their dwelling-places were so much alike."

37 Mencius said: "To feed people without showing them love – that is to treat them like pigs. To love people without showing them reverence – that is to keep them like pets. But honor and reverence are gifts not yet given. Honor and reverence without substance – you can't lure the noble-minded with such empty gestures."

38 Mencius said: "Our appearance belongs to the nature of Heaven. Only as a true sage can you abide by your appearance."

39 When Emperor Hsüan of Ch'i wanted to shorten his mourning period, Kung-sun Ch'ou said: "A year of mourning is better than none at all, isn't it?"

"That's like watching someone twist an elder's arm and saying: *Gently. Do it gently,*" replied Mencius. "What you should do is teach him how to honor parents and elders."

At the same time, there was a prince whose mother had died. On the prince's behalf, his teacher asked that he be allowed a mourning period of several months. "What do you think of that?" asked Kung-sun Ch'ou.

"The prince wants to observe the full mourning period," replied Mencius, "but he cannot. In this case, even a single day is better than nothing. There was nothing preventing Emperor Hsüan from mourning: he just wanted to avoid it."

40 Mencius said: "The noble-minded teach in five ways. They transform like rain coming in its season. They

realize Integrity. They perfect talents. They answer questions. They cultivate themselves and so stand apart as examples. These five ways are how the noble-minded teach."

41 Kung-sun Ch'ou said: "The Way is lofty and beautiful indeed, but it's like climbing to Heaven: it seems impossible to reach. Why not offer something people can hope to reach, something they can work at day after day with untiring diligence?"

"A great carpenter doesn't abandon the measuring string to make woodwork easy for inept apprentices," replied Mencius. "And Yi didn't give up a strong full draw to make archery easy for inept students. The noble-minded draw the bow and hold it. Then it seems they've leapt into the center of the Way, letting whoever is able follow them there."

42 Mencius said: "When all beneath Heaven abides in the Way, people use the Way to find themselves. When all beneath Heaven ignores the Way, people use themselves to find the Way. I never hear of using the Way to find the human anymore."

43 Adept Kung-tu said: "When T'eng Keng was your disciple, he seemed a man deserving of the Ritual respect, but you refused to answer his questions. Why?"

"When people wield such privileged positions as renown or wisdom, age or merit or friendship," replied Mencius, "I never answer them. And T'eng Keng wielded two of them."

44 Mencius said: "If someone stops where they should not, they'll stop anywhere. If someone slights a person they should treat generously, they'll slight anyone. And if someone races ahead, they retreat in a hurry."

45 Mencius said: "The noble-minded love things, but don't treat them with Humanity. They treat the people with Humanity, but don't treat them as kindred. Once you treat kindred as kindred, you treat the people with Humanity. And once you treat the people with Humanity, you love things."

46 Mencius said: "The wise understand all things, and so devote themselves to the essentials. The Humane

love all things, and so consider kindred devotion to the sages essential. The wisdom of Yao and Shun was that they didn't treat all things alike: they devoted themselves to essentials first. And the Humanity of Yao and Shun was that they didn't love all people alike: they devoted themselves to kindred affection for the sages.

"To be meticulous about mourning for a few months while declining to mourn the full three years, to ask about the etiquette of dining while swilling soup and wolfing down food – such things are called not understanding the essentials."

XIV

TO FATHOM THE MIND *Book Two*

1 Mencius said: "Emperor Hui of Liang was utterly Inhumane. The Humane extend their love to those they hate. The Inhumane inflict their hatred on those they love."

"What do you mean by that?" asked Kung-sun Ch'ou.

"In his passion for more territory, Emperor Hui sent his people to war, tearing them asunder and suffering disastrous defeats. Soon he wanted to return to the battlefield, but was afraid he couldn't win. So he sent his beloved son to the grave too.[1] This is what I mean by *inflicting their hatred on those they love.*"

2 Mencius said: "There were no just wars in *The Spring and Autumn Annals.* Some were better than others, but that's all. A sovereign may discipline his august lords by attacking them. But one country should never discipline another in such a way."

3 Mencius said: "If people believe everything in *The Book of History,* it's worse than having no *Book of History* at all. In the entire 'War Successfully Completed' chapter, I accept no more than two or three strips.[2]

"The Humane have no match in all beneath Heaven. If a Humane ruler attacks an Inhumane one, how could *blood flow so deep fulling sticks*[3] *begin floating away*?"

4 Mencius said: "There are people who say: *I am an expert in war and tactics.* But they're just common criminals. If the ruler of a country loves Humanity, he will have no match in all beneath Heaven. When he marches south, the northern tribes will complain: *Why does he leave us for last?* And when he marches east, the western tribes will complain: *Why does he leave us for last?*

"When Emperor Wu marched against Shang with three hundred war-chariots and three thousand illustrious warriors, he said: *Have no fear: I bring you peace. The Shang people are not my enemy.* At this, the Shang people bowed to the ground like animals shaking their horns loose. Hence, to invade was to rectify. People all want to rectify themselves, so what's the use of war?"

5 Mencius said: "A master carpenter or carriage-maker can hand down compass and square to his followers, but he cannot make them skillful."

6 Mencius said: "When Shun was eating cracked rice and wild greens, he lived as if he would spend his whole life like that. And when he was the Son of Heaven, wearing embroidered robes and playing his *ch'in* in the company of Yao's two daughters, he lived as if he'd always enjoyed such things."

7 Mencius said: "Only now have I realized the true gravity of killing a man's family members. If you kill his father, he'll kill your father. If you kill his brother, he'll kill your brother. There's precious little difference between that and killing your father or brother with your own hands."

8 Mencius said: "In ancient times, border stations were set up to resist attacks. Now they're set up to launch attacks."

9 Mencius said: "If you don't practice the Way yourself, how will you ever get your wife and child to practice it? And if you don't employ people according to the Way, how can you ever get your wife and child to practice it?"

10 Mencius said: "If you're always cultivating profit, you'll avoid death in bad years. If you're always cultivating Integrity, you'll avoid confusion in evil times."

11 Mencius said: "If you love renown, you can give away a nation of a thousand war-chariots. If you don't, you can't give away a basket of rice or bowl of soup without looking pained."

12 Mencius said: "If the worthy and Humane are not trusted, the country is an empty shell. If Ritual and Duty are ignored, leaders and citizens are confounded. And if the work of government is ignored, no amount of wealth will satisfy a country's needs."

13 Mencius said: "It has happened that Inhumane tyrants have gained control of a country. But such men have never ruled all beneath Heaven."

14 Mencius said: "The people are the most precious of all things. Next come the gods of soil and grain. The sovereign matters least.

"That's why a person must win over the people to become the Son of Heaven, win over the Son of Heaven to become an august lord, and win over an august lord to become a high minister.

"When an august lord neglects the gods of soil and grain, he should be replaced. When the sacrificial animals are perfect, the vessels of grain pure, the sacrifices observed in their proper seasons, and still drought and flood plague the land, then the gods of soil and grain should be replaced."

15 Mencius said: "A sage is teacher to the hundred generations. Po Yi and Liu-hsia Hui are such men. That's why the greedy are cured of greed when they hear the legend of Po Yi, and the timid grow resolute; why the niggardly grow generous when they hear the legend of Liu-

hsia Hui, and small minds grow broad. They arose a hundred generations ago, but a hundred generations from now they'll still inspire all who hear of them. If they weren't sages, how could this happen? And imagine what they meant to the people who knew them!"

16 Mencius said: "Humanity is the human. Put them together and you have the Way."

17 Mencius said: "When Confucius left Lu, he said: *There's no hurry, no hurry at all.* That's the Way to leave your parents' country. When he left Ch'i, he simply emptied his rice steamer and set out. That's the Way to leave a foreign land."

18 Mencius said: "When Confucius suffered such hardship in Ch'en and Ts'ai,[4] it was because he had no friends among rulers and ministers."

19 Mo Chi said: "I've never been much good at talk."

"There's no harm in that," replied Mencius. "Thoughtful people despise those who talk too much. The *Songs* say:

> *My troubled heart is grief-stricken*
> *at this small-minded world's hatred.*

Confucius was like that. And Emperor Wen was like this:

> *Though he couldn't ease their hatred,*
> *his renown never faltered among them."*

20 Mencius said: "The wise and worthy used their bright insight to open bright insight in people. Now pundits use blind ignorance to open bright insight in people."

21 Mencius said to Adept Kao: "If a footpath in the mountains suddenly gets a lot of use, it becomes a road. And if it's never used, it's soon choked with underbrush. That's how it is with your heart: choked with underbrush."

22 Adept Kao said: "Yü's music was much finer than Emperor Wen's."

"Why do you say that?" asked Mencius.

"Because the bell-pivots in his orchestra were nearly worn through."

"That's hardly proof. Do the deep ruts passing through a city gate come from the power of a single team of horses?"

23 When there was famine in Ch'i, Adept Ch'en said: "The Ch'i people are hoping you can get T'ang to open its granaries for them again. But you can't do that, can you?"

"If I did," replied Mencius, "I'd be another Feng Fu. Feng Fu was a man in Chin who was good at seizing tigers, but eventually became a good official. Many years later he went out into the country and found a crowd of people chasing a tiger. They cornered the tiger against some cliffs, but no one dared tangle with it. When they saw Feng Fu, they ran to greet him. And seeing him boldly roll up his sleeves and climb out of his carriage, they were delighted. But the other scholars there only laughed."

24 Mencius said: "The mouth's relation to flavor, the eye's to color, the ear's to sound, the nose's to fragrance, the four limbs' to ease – these are human nature. But they're also the Mandate of Heaven, so the noble-minded never call them human nature.

"Humanity's relation to father and son, Duty's to sovereign and minister, Ritual's to guest and host, understanding's to the wise and worthy, the sage's to Heaven's Way – these are the Mandate of Heaven. But they're also human nature, so the noble-minded never call them the Mandate of Heaven."

25 Hao-sheng Pu-hai asked: "What kind of man is Adept Yüeh-cheng?"

"A man of virtue and sincerity," replied Mencius.

"What do you mean by *virtue* and *sincerity*?"

"What we aspire to is called *virtue,* and to possess it within us is called *sincerity,*" began Mencius. "To possess it in rich abundance is called *beauty,* and to be ablaze with that rich abundance is called *great*. Someone transformed by that greatness is a *sage,* and to be a sage beyond all knowing – that is called *divinity*. Yüeh-cheng has mastered the first two, but the last four are still beyond him."

26 Mencius said: "When people abandon the school of Mo Tzu, they turn to Yang Chu. And when they abandon the school of Yang Chu, they turn to Confucius. When they turn to our Confucian school, we should take them in. That's all.

"But these days, people debate the followers of Mo Tzu and Yang Chu, and it's like they're chasing stray pigs. First they herd them back into the pen, then they tie up their legs."

27 Mencius said: "There are three forms of taxation: cloth, grain, and labor. The noble-minded levy one, and relax the other two. If you levy two at once, the people starve and die. If you levy all three at once, father and son are torn asunder."

28 Mencius said: "An august lord has three treasures: land, people, and government. If they treasure pearls and jade, they're destined for ruin."

29 When P'en-ch'eng K'uo took office in Ch'i, Mencius said: "He's as good as dead."

Eventually P'en-ch'eng K'uo was put to death, and the disciples asked: "How did you know he'd be put to death?"

"He was a man of little talent," replied Mencius, "and he'd never learned the great noble-minded Way. That's all it took to kill him."

30 When Mencius went to T'eng and stayed in the Upper Palace, there was a half-finished pair of sandals on the windowsill. At some point, the palace servants came looking for them but couldn't find them. So someone asked: "Can your followers really be so shameless?"

"Do you think we came all this way just to steal sandals?" replied Mencius.

"I wouldn't think so. But as a teacher, you don't chase after students who leave and you don't refuse students who come. If they come to you with an earnest mind, you accept them without any question."

31 Mencius said: "There are things people find unbearable. To see that and use it to understand what makes life bearable – that is Humanity. There are things people will not do. To see that and use it to understand what people should do – that is Duty.

"The heart detests harming others. If you apply that everywhere, you'll never exhaust Humanity. The heart detests peeking through holes and stealing over walls. If you apply that everywhere, you'll never exhaust Duty. People resent condescension. If you apply that everywhere, you can practice Duty wherever you go.

"To say what you should not say – that is to use words as a ploy. Not to say what you should say – that is to use silence as a ploy. Either way, it's no different from peeking through holes and stealing over walls."

32 Mencius said: "Words that speak of things close at hand and carry far-reaching implications – those are the good words. Guarding the essentials and applying them broadly – that is the good Way.

"The noble-minded always use forthright words, so the Way endures in them. And they cultivate themselves tenaciously, so all beneath Heaven is at peace.

"People keep leaving their own fields to weed the fields of others. It's a sickness. They demand everything of others, and nothing of themselves."

33 Mencius said: "For Yao and Shun, it was their very nature. And T'ang and Wu – they returned to it.

"When every movement of mind and body is in accord with Ritual – that is the fullest form of Integrity. When you mourn the dead utterly, it isn't to impress the living. When you abide by Integrity without swerving, it isn't to earn a fat salary. And when you speak with true sincerity, always standing by your word, it isn't to justify your actions. The noble-minded simply put the law into action, then await their fate."

34 Mencius said: "When you counsel great figures, do it with disdain. Don't let their majesty impress you. Ceilings thirty feet high and rafter-beams a yard across – if I realized my every dream, I wouldn't have such things. Serving girls by the hundred and tables ten feet wide spread with food – if I realized my every dream, I wouldn't have such things. Great fun drinking, riding, and hunting, always a retinue of a thousand carriages following behind – if I realized my every dream, I wouldn't have such things.

"The things they do are all things I would never do. And the things I do are all in accordance with the ancient precepts. So why should I cower before them?"

35 Mencius said: "For nurturing the mind, there's nothing like paring your desires away to a very few. If you have few desires, there may still be some capricious whims in your mind, but they'll be few. If you have many desires, there may still be some enduring principles in your mind, but they'll be few indeed."

36 Tseng Hsi loved sheep-dates. But his son, Master Tseng, couldn't bear to eat them.

"Which tastes better – roast mincemeat or sheep-dates?" asked Kung-sun Ch'ou.

"Roast mincemeat, of course," replied Mencius.

"Then why did Master Tseng eat roast mincemeat and not sheep-dates?"

"Roast mincemeat is a taste shared by many, but a taste for sheep-dates is unique. It's forbidden to use someone's personal name, but not their family name. This is because a family name is shared by many, while a personal name is unique."

37 Adept Wan Chang asked: "When he was in Ch'en, Confucius said: *Let's go back home. The young in our villages are full of impetuous ambition. They forge ahead but cannot forget their childish ways.*[5] But he was in Ch'en, so what made him think of the impetuous young scholars in Lu?"

Mencius replied: "Confucius said: *I can't find students who steer the middle Way, so I turn to the impetuous and the timid. The impetuous forge ahead, and the timid know what to avoid.*[6] Obviously, Confucius wanted to find students who steer the middle Way. But since he couldn't find such people, he started thinking about the best alternatives."

"What sort of person did he mean by *impetuous*?" asked Wan Chang.

"People like Ch'in Chang, Tseng Hsi, and Mu P'i."

"Why did he call them impetuous?"

"They were full of ambition," said Mencius, "and grand boasting about *The ancients! The ancients!* But if you examine their actions, you see they often violated the ancient precepts.

"And when he couldn't find the impetuous for students, all Confucius could do is look for arrogant scholars who wouldn't condescend to anything the least bit impure. These are the timid, and they are the next best alternative."

Wan Chang continued: "Confucius said: *I regret all those*

who pass by my gate without entering to become students – all but the righteous villager. A righteous villager is the thief of Integrity.[7] What sort of person did he mean by *righteous villager?*"

"All that grand boasting of the impetuous is senseless," replied Mencius. "Their words ignore their actions; their actions ignore their words. And still they bluster about *The ancients! The ancients!* And how can the timid walk around so cold and self-contained? They live in this world, so they should act like they're a part of it. But if these two only act with virtue and benevolence, they're alright.

"As for those righteous villagers: they enfeeble themselves fawning all over this world."

"If a whole village praises someone as righteous," said Adept Wan, "then they'd be called righteous wherever they went. So why did Confucius call such a person *the thief of Integrity?*"

"If you want to accuse such a person, there's no place to begin," replied Mencius. "If you want to criticize, there's nothing to criticize. They do what everyone else does, in perfect harmony with this sordid world. They live that way, and yet seem loyal and sincere. They act that way, and yet seem pure and honest. They please everyone and believe they're always right. But it's impossible to enter the Way of Yao and Shun with them. That's why Confucius called such a person *the thief of Integrity.*

"Confucius said:

> *I hate things that are not what they appear. I hate weeds for fear they'll be confused with young rice. I hate sweet talk for fear it will be confused with eloquence. I hate calculating tongues for fear they'll be confused with sincerity. I hate the dissolute songs of Cheng for fear they'll be confused with music. I hate purple for fear it will be confused with the purity of vermilion. And I hate righteous villagers for fear they'll be confused with people of Integrity.*

"The noble-minded simply return to the changeless principle. When the changeless principle is established, the people flourish. And when the people flourish, the twisty ways of evil are unknown."

38 Mencius said: "It was over five hundred years from Yao and Shun to T'ang. People like Yü and Kao Yao understood because they knew Yao and Shun, and people like T'ang understood through learning. It was over five hundred years from T'ang to Emperor Wen. People like Yi Yin and Lai Chu understood because they knew T'ang, and people like Emperor Wen understood through learning. It was over five hundred years from Emperor Wen to Confucius. People like Duke T'ai and San-yi Sheng understood be-

cause they knew Wen, and people like Confucius understood through learning.

"Now it's hardly been a hundred years from Confucius to our own age. We aren't far from his time, and we're so near his home. But if no one here's gleaned anything from that great sage, then no one here's gleaned anything."

Notes

I. Emperor Hui of Liang Book One

1 **miles:** The Chinese mile *(li)* is much shorter than our own, the ratio being 3 *li* per mile.

2 **Humanity:** See Key Terms: *Jen.*

3 **Duty:** See Key Terms: *Yi.*

4 **Emperor Wen:** Father of Wu, the founder of the Chou Dynasty, Wen was considered responsible for the resplendent culture of the Chou Dynasty, hence his name, which means "culture." See Historical Table.

5 **acre:** The Chinese acre *(mu)* is much smaller than our own, the ratio being 6.6 *mu* per acre or less.

6 **square miles:** In ancient China this form of measurement seems to have meant something different than it does for us. Seven hundred square miles apparently means an area of land seven hundred miles on each side. Still, such measurements don't seem consistent, and seem more figurative than literal.

7 **Emperor Hsiang:** Emperor Hui died, and Hsiang was the son who became his successor.

8 **Duke Huan:** Most illustrious of the noble lords in the earlier years of the Chou Dynasty (reigned 685–643). See note III.2.

9 **Integrity:** See Key Terms: *Te.*

10 **Middle Kingdom:** Ancient heartland in the north inhabited by fully civilized Chinese, as opposed to the southern and other outlying regions, which were "barbarian" or only partially civilized. As those regions became fully Chinese, this term *(Chung Kuo)* extended to mean all of China.

11 **Ritual:** See Key Terms: *Li.*

II. Emperor Hui of Liang Book Two

1 **Way:** See Key Terms: *Tao.*

2 **Emperor T'ai:** Chou sovereign who preceded King Wen. See Historical Table.

3 **Celestial Lord:** Shang Ti, the Shang Dynasty's supreme deity: see Introduction p. xi f.

4 **Emperor Wu:** Chou Emperor who conquered the last Shang emperor and replaced the Shang Dynasty with the Chou Dynasty. Hence his name, which means "martial." See Historical Table.

5 **Ch'i:** Different from the Ch'i ruled by King Hsüan.

6 **Emperor Kung Liu:** Chou sovereign in a time well before the Chou state conquered the Shang Dynasty, when the semi-barbarian Chou was being forced east toward Shang by western tribes.

7 **Tyrant Chieh . . . Tyrant Chou:** Chieh and Chou were the last, debased rulers of the Hsia and Shang dynasties respectively. In overthrowing them, T'ang and Wu founded new and noble dynasties: the Shang and Chou, respectively.

8 **Ch'i invaded the nation of Yen:** Trying to make himself look like the sage-emperor Yao, who passed over his own

son and bequeathed the throne to the most worthy successor, Emperor K'uai of Yen abdicated in favor of his prime minister, Lord Chih, in 315 B.C.E. The prime minister was expected to decline, but instead accepted. This sparked a very destructive civil war led by the rightful heir, and King Hsüan of Ch'i finally intervened. See also IV.8–9.

9 **Master Tseng:** Disciple of Confucius who became an influential teacher.

10 **Ch'i Mountain:** See next section for the entire story.

III. Kung-Sun Ch'ou Book One

1 **Kung-sun Chou:** Disciple of Mencius.

2 **successes of Kuan Chung:** Duke Huan became sovereign in Ch'i by killing his brother Chiu. Kuan Chung was initially Chiu's advisor, but afterwards became a sage prime minister under Duke Huan. His talents turned Ch'i into a powerful and rich state, and made Huan first among the august lords.

3 **Duke Chou:** A cultural hero much admired by Confucius and Mencius, Duke Chou helped his brother, Wu, found the Chou Dynasty. He was also a major intellectual figure: As the primary architect of the Chou political system, he set up the institutions of sagely government and is traditionally credited with developing the doctrine of the Mandate of Heaven, which introduced ethics into government (see Historical Table and Introduction, pp. xii–xiii).

4 **Mind:** The word *hsin,* which recurs throughout this section, means both "heart" and "mind." The Chinese made no fundamental distinction between the two.

5 **Meng Pin:** Courageous warrior of antiquity.

6 **Master Kao:** Philosopher contemporary with Mencius. See XI.1–6 for their dialogues on human nature.

7 **ch'i:** The universal breath-force or vital energy.

8 **Tsai Yü, Adept Kung . . . Jan Po-niu, Min Tzu-ch'ien, and Yen Hui:** These five were disciples of Confucius.

9 **Po Yi:** Po Yi and his brother Shu Ch'i (twelfth century B.C.E.) were heir to the throne, but they felt it would be wrong to accept it, so they refused. As a result, they lived in great poverty, finally dying of cold and hunger in the mountains.

10 **Yi Yin:** The great minister who helped T'ang found the Shang Dynasty. See Historical Table.

11 **Yao . . . Shun:** Two mythic sage-emperors from legendary prehistory. See Historical Table.

12 **disparage me:** *Songs* 155. A bird is speaking.

13 **"T'ai Chia":** *The Analects* IV.1.

14 **Liu-hsia Hui:** Sage governor in Lu (7th–6th century).

IV. Kung-Sun Ch'ou Book Two

1 **Shen T'ung:** For an explanation of the events referred to in this and the following section, see note II.7.

2 **Ch'en Chia:** One of the Ch'i emperor's counselors.

3 **Master Szu:** The celebrated grandson of Confucius and reputed author of *The Doctrine of the Mean,* one of the Confucian classics. Mencius is said to have studied under one of Master Szu's disciples.

V. Duke Wen of T'eng Book One

1 **Yen Hui:** Perhaps the most able of Confucius' disciples. Confucius admired his wisdom and ability above all others and grieved deeply when he died young.

2 **mutual assistance:** In the personal system *(kung),* each family cultivated its own land and paid ten percent of the produce as a tax. In the mutual system *(chu),* each family cultivated its own land, and also cultivated public land jointly with other families. The produce of the public land was paid as a tax. This is essentially the well-field system described below. In the communal system *(ch'e),* families cultivated land communally, dividing the produce between them and paying ten percent to the government.

3 **well-field system:** Under this system, each parcel of land is divided into nine plots and so looks like the character *(ching)* meaning *well:* 井. The eight outer plots in this configuration are each cultivated by one family. In addition to cultivating their own plot, the eight families cultivate the center plot jointly. This is public land, and its produce is given to the government as a tax.

4 **Shen Nung:** literally: "Divine Farmer," a mythic emperor believed to have reigned from 2838 to 2698 B.C.E., is credited with the invention of the plow and the agricultural arts. He also discovered the medicinal uses of plants, and began the practice of trading in markets.

5 **Kao Yao:** Shun's sage justice minister.

6 **Mo Tzu:** Mo Tzu (5th c. B.C.E.), who lived in the century be-

tween Confucius and Mencius, was the founder of a major school of social philosophy that competed with the Confucian school. He is most famously associated with the idea that social ills can be resolved if we each love all others equally, rather than loving some (family, e.g.) more than others.

VI. Duke Wen of T'eng Book Two

1 **Ch'en Tai:** Disciple of Mencius.

2 **summons:** See X.7 for a fuller version of this story.

3 **Ching Ch'un:** Politician in the time of Mencius.

4 **Kung-sun Yen and Chang Yi:** Itinerant scholars who were very influential as advisors of rulers.

5 **boundless dwelling-place:** That is: Humanity. See XIII.33 and 36.

6 **token of credentials:** Each government rank had its own prescribed token. Itinerant scholars wanting a position would present this token to a sovereign as a way of proving their qualifications.

7 **P'eng Keng:** Disciple of Mencius.

8 **Wan Chang:** Disciple of Mencius.

9 **K'uang Chang:** High official in Ch'i.

VII. Li Lou Book One

1 **Three Dynasties:** Hsia, Shang, Chou.

2 **I rinse my feet clean:** This song also appears in "The Fisherman," part of the ancient *Ch'u Tz'u* anthology *(The Songs of the South).*

3 **Duke T'ai:** Duke T'ai became a great counselor to Emperors Wen and Wu, helping them to overcome the Shang tyrant and found the Chou Dynasty.

4 **Jan Ch'iu:** Disciple of Confucius.

5 **Chun-yü K'un:** Scholar who rose to high position from humble origins.

VIII. Li Lou Book Two

1 **Lord Ch'an:** Wise and worthy prime minister of Cheng much admired by Confucius.

2 **from the people:** The poems in the *Book of Songs* were folk songs gathered by emperors wanting to know how the people felt about their rule.

3 **without entering:** See V.4.

4 **wise and worthy:** See *The Analects* VI.10.

IX. Wan Chang Book One

1 **ch'in:** An ancient stringed instrument played by all intellectuals in ancient China, ancestor to the more familiar Japanese koto.

2 **Hsien-chiu Meng:** Disciple of Mencius.

3 **half a person left:** There is nothing in the language itself to show that this is describing a future possibility, so it could literally be read in the present: "there *isn't* half a person left."

4 **T'ai Chia:** Son who suceeded T'ang after his death.

XII. Master Kao Book Two

1 **Wu Huo:** A legendary strongman.

2 **better even than Yü:** For Yü managing floodwaters, see V.4 and VI.9.

XIII. To Fathom the Mind Book One

1 **Yi Yin banished T'ai Chia:** See IX.6.

XIV. To Fathom the Mind Book Two

1 **beloved son to the grave:** See also I.5.

2 **two or three strips:** Books were written on bamboo strips, which were tied together with leather string.

3 **fulling sticks:** Used by women as they prepared heavy winter clothes. In literary use, it usually implies the men have been conscripted and are far away at war.

4 **hardship in Ch'en and Ts'ai:** See *The Analects* XI.2 and XV.2.

5 **childish ways:** Cf. *The Analects* V.21.

6 **what to avoid:** *The Analects* XIII.21.

7 **thief of Integrity:** This sentence is *The Analects* XVII.11.

Historical Table

Emperors

LEGENDARY PERIOD

Yao

Shun

——————————————— 2200 B.C.E.

Yü

HSIA DYNASTY

Tyrant Chieh

——————————————— 1766

T'ang

(Yi Yin)

SHANG DYNASTY

Tyrant Chou

——————————————— 1122

CHOU STATE

T'ai

Wen

Wu

Wu ← Wu

(Duke Chou)

CHOU DYNASTY

Confucius (551–479)

Warring States Period (403–221)

Mencius (4th c.)

——————————————— 221

CH'IN DYNASTY

——————————————— 206

HAN DYNASTY

Key Terms

An Outline of Mencius' Thought

Li: 禮 Ritual

A religious concept associated with the worship of gods and spirits prior to Confucius, Ritual was reconfigured by Confucius to mean the web of social responsibilities that bind a society together. These include the proprieties in virtually all social interactions, and are determined by the individual's position within the structure of society. By calling these secular acts "Ritual," Confucius makes everyday experience itself a sacred realm. This Ritual structure of society is part of a vast cosmological weave: the Ritual structure of natural process as the ten thousand things emerge from the primal emptiness.

Jen: 仁 Humanity (Humane)

The character for *jen* is formed by a combination of the characters for "human being" and "two," and it means all of the moral qualities expressed in the behavior of ideal human beings toward one another. *Jen* is the internalization of *li,* and *li* is the codified external expression of *jen.* So, to be Humane means to master a kind of selflessness by which we dwell as an integral part of the Ritual weave. Or, more simply: to act with a selfless and reverent concern for the well-being of others. *Jen* is the touchstone of Confucian sagehood, a kind of enlightenment which Confucius claimed was beyond even him.

Yi: 義 Duty

The prescriptions of Ritual are general in nature. The ability to apply them in specific situations is Duty, and so Duty is the particular ethical expression of Humanity.

Tao: 道 Way

The effortless process of human society functioning according to its natural Ritual structure. It can be expanded to cover Ritual's cosmological dimensions, making it comparable to the more familiar Taoist Tao. Hence: the effortless process of the cosmos functioning according to its natural Ritual structure. The cosmos always abides by the Tao, with the frequent exception of human societies.

Te: 德 Integrity

The ability to act according to the Way. Or more precisely, the embodiment of the Tao in the sage, where it becomes a kind of power through which the sage can transform others "by example."

T'ien 天 Heaven

Natural process. Or, more descriptively, the inevitable unfolding of things in the cosmological process. Hence, Heaven appears as a kind of immanent fate in the human realm – and as Ritual is its organizing principle, it becomes a kind of moral force encouraging societies to abide by Ritual and the Tao.

Further Reading

Chan Wing-tsit. *A Source Book of Chinese Philosophy.* New York: Columbia University Press, 1969.

Confucius. *The Analects.* Translated by David Hinton. Washington, D.C.: Counterpoint, 1998.

DeBary, William T., Wing-tsit Chan, and Burton Watson, eds. *Sources of Chinese Tradition.* 2 vols. New York: Columbia University Press, 1960.

Eno, Robert. *The Confucian Creation of Heaven.* Buffalo: SUNY Press, 1990.

Fingarette, Herbert. *Confucius: The Secular As Sacred.* New York: Harper & Row, 1972.

Fung Yu-lan. *A History of Chinese Philosophy.* Translated by Derk Bodde. Princeton: Princeton University Press, 1952–53.

Graham, A. C. *Disputers of the Tao.* LaSalle, Ill.: Open Court, 1989.

Hughes, E.R. *The Great Learning and the Mean in Action.* London: Dent, 1942.

Mencius. *Mencius.* Translated by D. C. Lau. London: Penguin, 1970.

———. *Mencius, Vol. 1, The Chinese Classics.* Translated by James Legge. 1861–73. Reprint Hong Kong: University of Hong Kong Press, 1960.

Mote, Frederick. *Intellectual Foundations of China.* New York: Alfred A. Knopf, 1971.

Ropp, Paul, ed. *Heritage of China*. Berkeley: University of California Press, 1990.

Schwartz, Benjamin. *The World of Thought in Ancient China*. Cambridge: Harvard University Press, 1985.

Shun Kwong-Loi. *Mencius and Early Chinese Thought*. Palo Alto, Calif.: Stanford University Press, 1997.

Tu Wei-ming. *Humanity and Self-Cultivation: Essays in Confucian Thought*. Berkeley: Asian Humanities Press, 1979.